"Tunnel 13"

The Story of the DeAutremont Brothers
and
The West's Last Great Train Hold up

By Art Chipman

Pine Cone Publishers
2251 Ross Lane
Medford, Oregon 97501

Library of Congress Catalog Card Number: 77-075859
International Standard Book Number: 0-912720-05-0

CONTENTS

ILLUSTRATIONS

Acknowledgements

My appreciation for assistance in preparation of this book is necessarily spread in many areas. The great help of Mrs. Edward C. Kelly (Mary Greiner) saved me untold hours of research, and her willingness to discuss the case and the people involved gave a background and flavor not otherwise obtainable. Her superb coverage of the trial as a young newspaper reporter and subsequent interviews with the various principals were absolutely invaluable as a research source. I am certain I could not have obtained some of the pictures and information without her tremendous assistance.

Justin Smith, District Attorney for Jackson County, deserves my special thanks for providing the confessions of the three boys and several pictures. The use of this material for reference purposes over a prolonged period of time made my project much easier.

Jackson County Sheriff Duane Franklin was most helpful in providing a number of unpublished letters and other items.

The *Medford Mail Tribune* graciously gave me unlimited permission to quote from their copyrighted material, as well as permitting me total access to their microfilm library of back issues. This was very important to my undertaking.

I sincerely thank W. M. (Bill) Robertson, with the Southern Pacific Company in San Francisco, for his fine cooperation in providing numerous and pertinent pictures.

W. J. Cotter, Chief Postal Inspector, provided some extremely worthwhile information for the viewpoint of the U.S. Post Office, including pictures.

The Ironton *Evening Tribune* (Ironton, Ohio) was most cooperative in permitting me access to its files.

Robert Becker, of the Bancroft Library at U.C. Berkeley, was tremendously cooperative, and I am indebted to the Bancroft Library for permission to search through the Southern Pacific files in their possession. This is the source for much of the information relative to the details in the search for the fugitives.

The Jacksonville (Oregon) Museum staff was extremely helpful to me in obtaining some very worthwhile material.

Numerous individuals who resided in Southern Oregon at the time either of the crime or trial, or who had some scrap of information, were interviewed, and while I cannot name them all in these credits, they certainly aided me greatly and I thank them.

Foreword

One of the most bizarre crimes of all time took place on a Fall day of 1923, in the remote Siskiyou Mountains of Southern Oregon. Three young brothers' unsuccessful attempt to rob a Southern Pacific Express resulted in the brutal slaying of four trainmen. Following the tragedy, one of the greatest man hunts in all the world, up to that time, was launched. Nevertheless, for almost four years, the search was fruitless.

It was the single crime the boys were to commit, but following their capture they were swept into a maelstrom of hate, virtually becoming political pawns, and their crime a "cause celebre". While the event took place more than 50 years ago, the name of the DeAutremont brothers is still a household word in many parts of the West.

This is the story of that tragic happening and the bitter rendezvous with destiny for the three young men, seemingly born under a crossed star, with sorrow and tragedy tagging their footsteps, and blighting the lives of many who loved or befriended them.

I am certain that, even after all these years, this book will continue to arouse long-smoldering hates and passions. In 1973, I participated in a 90 minute special program about the DeAutremonts on KMED-TV and received a rash of unkind cards and letters criticizing me for not being more harsh in my judgment and discussion of the brothers and their crime. While I in no way condone the vicious, senseless slayings or the motives of the crime, in some ways I feel the greatest crime the three committed was their failure to recant publicly and express regret for the whole sad affair. Forgiveness under those circumstances is very difficult for many people.

As the author, I would like to emphasize that whatever other faults this book may contain, I have sincerely endeavored to make it historically accurate. Any quotations used are actual printed quotes from definite sources—and if some of those sources were using their own imaginations at the time, this is now impossible to ascertain. Among the major problems of its writing were the numerous conflicting statements. Some of these were obvious errors promulgated by careless writers with inadequate information and active imaginations. Others were different views obtained from the same hazy sources but with contrary interpretations. A half century has dimmed many memories, and this too has created various versions

of certain happenings. I have diligently tried to sort out the accurate facts through interviews with many people (including the former Hazel DeAutremont and Jackie Hugh DeAutremont), and I have drawn on innumerable newspaper articles in Oregon and Ohio, together with countless other writings of the period and since. Despite some previous articles which differ in their presentation, I believe the following is as accurate as possible account of what took place.

Some people may feel I have skipped over many family details of later years, and this is a correct assumption. In my opinion, these details were not important and might bring undue anguish to persons who have already suffered sufficiently. There are many individuals still living in the Pacific Northwest, bearing the name of DeAutremont, who are splendid citizens and a thorough credit to their communities. This book should in no manner be a reflection upon them, rather, it should be considered a valuable object lesson to young people of the life-long consequences of one day's ill conceived actions.

Chapter 1

A Train is Held Up

It was 12:42 p.m. on October 11, 1923, when Southern Pacific's train # 13, the crack "Shasta Limited", whistled a ringing highball and slowly puffed up the mountain from the regular stop at tiny Siskiyou, Oregon. A short distance ahead was tunnel # 13, destined to be one of the most memorable sites on the vast S. P. system, as the scene of the last great train hold up in the West. It was also one of the bloodiest, and was followed by the greatest man hunt ever conducted by the U.S. Post Office Department and the Special Agents of the Southern Pacific Railroad.

Tunnel # 13 is a few miles south of the small town of Ashland, Oregon, with the tiny lumbering community of Hilts,* California, several miles farther on. Piercing the rugged tree-covered Siskiyou Mountains 3,108 feet in a northeast to southwest direction, the tunnel emerges on the southern face of the mountain. In 1923, few roads penetrated the remote area and the rare, isolated mountain shacks were widely scattered. The steep ridges were blanketed by heavy timber and thick brush, making travel by foot extremely difficult.

Originating in Portland, train # 13 frequently carried a valuable load of mail and was often referred to as the "Gold Special" although its treasure was generally highly exaggerated. On this date it consisted of four baggage cars, together with three coaches containing 86 passengers, in addition to 20 trainmen dead-heading their way to various points south . . . and a rendezvous with railroad history. It was a day which would be forever engraved in the memory of each person aboard and provide a subject of conversation for the remainder of their lifetimes.

A number of section hands were working within sight of the train but they paid little attention as Engineer Sidney L. Bates made the customary "air brake test" just before entering the long tunnel. This was to double check the proper functioning of the brakes prior to the lengthy, steep descent at the west exit. As the brakes were applied, around 500 feet from the entrance, the train slowed down

*Now, more commonly called Hilt.

to about 5 miles per hour, with the test being completed some two or three hundred feet from the tunnel when normal speed was resumed.

Picking up speed, train #13 entered the mouth of the tunnel and at that moment, two slender young men leaped from behind a clump of brush alongside the tracks and dashed for the train. If Sid Bates glanced back and saw them, he probably thought little about it, for thousands of men customarily hopped trains to obtain free transportation. And, although the railroad constantly tried to keep from hauling free riders, many of the trainmen paid little or no attention to these "bindle stiffs", as they were frequently called.

Had Mr. Bates dreamed of the tragedy destined during the following hour, he surely would have changed his routine somehow. All he did was throw the throttle wide open.

The younger of the two men quickly grabbed the iron ladder rungs and swung aboard, but his companion had trouble until a leg was helpfully stuck out for him to catch and pull himself aboard. Unseen by anyone at the time, a .45 Colt automatic slipped from the second man's belt and clattered along the track through the cinders and across the ties. The Mexican section hands still, apparently, had not noticed them, but then, fellows clinging to passing trains were not an uncommon sight.

Making their way forward in the semi-darkness of the tunnel, they finally reached the "blind baggage" (a recessed area at the rear of the tender). Here they crouched, discussed their next move, and decided that the younger, who still had his .45 automatic, would "take care" of the engineer while the older confronted the fireman. They crept up and over the tender, towards the engine cab, one nervously gripping his automatic, the other clutching a blackjack.

A few hundred feet from the tunnel exit, the two men leaped from out of the darkness into the cab, the younger jabbing the .45 menacingly at the engineer as he yelled, "Stop the train with the engine cab just clear of the tunnel. If you fail to do so the fireman will take your place because you will be dead". The other man barked at the fireman, "If the engineer fails to stop the train, with the cab just clear of the tunnel, you are to take his place because he will be dead".

Noting the obvious youthfulness of the two, the engineer almost smiled and apparently didn't take their threats too seriously, but, noting the pistol, he did follow the instructions and slowly the train ground to a stop. The cab barely protruded from the tunnel exit, sitting there, rumbling in powerful wheezes . . . the engine's "warning bell" ringing an ominous portent across the uninhabited mountainside.

The engineer observed a third youth, standing alongside the tracks, holding a repeating shotgun, with a pistol in his belt. The younger man ordered the engineer and fireman from the cab and

The express car interior shortly after the dynamiting which shows the still-smoking debris, along with the vertabrae of Railway Postal Clerk Dougherty, laid bare from the tremendous explosion.

herded them a few yards to the side. At that moment, Elvyn E. Dougherty, the mail clerk, slid open the door of the mail car and stuck his head out to see why the train was stopping. The youth with the shotgun quickly whirled and fired. Buckshot rattled along the side of the mail car, but apparently Dougherty was unharmed, for he slammed the door shut and locked it. The men yelled at him to open the door but he ignored them, little realizing what a terrible fate would befall him within the next few minutes.

In the baggage car, immediately behind the express car, Hugh Haffey also wondered why the train had stopped in the remote area. He too opened the door and peered out toward the engine. To his astonishment he saw men with guns pointed at the train crew standing with their hands in the air. Knowing he could do nothing, he quietly closed and locked the door to await further developments. They weren't long in coming.

One of the men darted over to the bank, grabbed up a heavy suitcase full of dynamite from behind some bushes and shoved it on the front of the mail car. Some extra sticks of dynamite were stacked on top of the suitcase, thec the men hurriedly followed the attached wires back over the bank to where a detonating machine had been hidden earlier.

The plunger was quickly rammed down and an ear-splitting blast punctured the mountain stillness, with clouds of dust and smoke boiling around the mouth of the tunnel. The explosion was followed by a pregnant silence, punctuated only by the yells of the three men, the hiss of escaping steam from the broken hoses and the continually ringing bell of the waiting engine. The two trainmen stood, hands in the air, stunned at what they were seeing.

The entire front end of the mail car had been ripped apart like a ruptured sardine can; however, the twisted sheets of steel gave only a slight indication of the total devastation within. The stove in the mail car had been demolished, throwing fire in every direction. Mail sacks were aflame and the fumes from the burning canvas combined with the pungent odor of the dynamite to form an unbreathable acrid mass of smoke. The neophyte robbers' excitement and inexperience with dynamite had resulted in the use of far too much explosive, which had not only destroyed the mail car and contents but actually raised the entire front end of the car from the track. When it settled back down, the air brake lines were ruptured causing an emergency lock on the wheels (this is a point of controversy as some sources claim two of the wheels dropped off to one side). In any event, the fact that the express car could not be moved was only the first of a chain of miscalculations that foiled the hold up attempt and turned the whole episode into a deadly Keystone Kops caper.

Churning masses of smoke and steam were pouring from the demolished mail car and the two railroad men stared hypnotized at what was taking place before their eyes. It was obvious that the mail clerk could not have lived through such a blast. Ironically, it had not been Dougherty's regularly scheduled run, but, as a favor for a friend who wanted to go deer hunting, he had traded shifts with John Edwards. The mighty explosion had also thundered Hugh Haffey into unconsciousness in his baggage car.

One of the robbers leaped into the mail car, stabbing a flashlight into the black maelstrom of smoke and steam. It was too thick; he could see nothing. Feeling his way along, eyes watering, he stumbled into the car but could not proceed. Returning to the front he jumped to the ground and dashed to the far end, where he began examining the coupling to see how it could be unhooked from the rest of the train and the express car pulled forward for looting.

At that moment, outside of the robbers, only the two crewmen still alive at the engine and the unconscious Haffey were aware a hold up was in progress. Farther back in the tunnel, numerous windows of the passenger cars had been shattered by the concussion and conductor J. O. Marrett was trying to comfort those injured by flying glass and reassure the unharmed. While some of the people were peering up the tunnel into the smoky darkness, none of them suspected the cause of the delay.

Charles Orin (Coyl) Johnson, a dead-heading brakeman, swung to the ground and started towards the engine. The conductor had gathered some fusees at the rear of the train and after lighting them, joined Johnson, Lowell S. Grim, the head brakeman, Samuel

Elvyn E. Dougherty, the Railway Postal Clerk, took the fatal run on train #13 as a favor for a friend.

L. Clayton and several others who were by then stumbling alongside the train toward the engine, trying to ascertain what had happened.

Upon sighting the demolished mail car and the clouds of acrid smoke pouring from it, Marrett assumed there had been an explosion of some sort and, afraid the open-fired fusees might ignite any gases still present, he and all except Johnson returned to the passenger cars to get flashlights.

Peering through the blinding, turbulent murkiness, Johnson went on, poking his red light into the darkness, vainly trying to see what was ahead. To his astonishment, from out of the swirling dust and steam, a young man suddenly appeared, pointing a pistol at him and telling him a robbery was in progress and his life was in great danger; that they were trying to get the mail car out of the tunnel and one false move on his part would mean death. Johnson saw the determined young man meant what he said and quickly agreed to help uncouple the car, but advised that the engine must be moved ahead as the release lever was lifted.

Feeling the brakeman could not be left unguarded, the robber ordered him to raise his hands in the air and go ahead to the engine and tell the men there to have the engineer pull forward while he

Top: Fireman Marvin L. Seng, a resident of Dunsmuir, was shot by Roy DeAutremont.

Center: Engineer Sidney L. Bates was the last of the four trainmen to be killed, shot in the head by Hugh just before the three brothers fled the scene of the crime.

Bottom: The buckshot-riddled body of Fireman "Coyl" Johnson.

held up the lever. In his fright and excitement, the brakeman apparently failed to remember to keep his hands in the air. As he and his red light suddenly emerged from the pall of dust and steam, the two nervous bandits at the engine jumped to the conclusion he must have killed the third one still concealed at the rear of the mail car. Both instinctively fired at him, with the shotgun slugs tearing into him simultaneously with a bullet from the .45 pistol.

Staggering forward towards one of his killers, the brakeman slowly crumbled to the ground, muttering "That other fellow said to pull the thing ahead", faithfully delivering the message which had cost him his life.

The youngest bandit ordered the now thoroughly apprehensive engineer to pull the express car ahead, but the engine's wheels would only spin, without moving the damaged express car. Dropping to his knees, one of the men tried to peer under the swirling smoke and steam, which was getting thicker and thicker and more acrid. (In his later recounting of what had occurred, he claimed the explosion had knocked some of the wheels off the track but railroad men disputed this.)

After several more futile attempts to move the engine and mail car, one of the men yelled, "We'll have to see if we can get anything out where it is, we can't get it out of the tunnel." After hurriedly examining the interior, they could see a big hole in the floor and the burning mail sacks; thick smoke blanked out everything else from view; parts of the dead mail clerk could be seen scattered around. They decided it would be at least an hour or more before it could possibly clear enough for them to enter the car and search out the valuables among the many sacks. By then, a posse from nearby Ashland would undoubtedly have reached the scene.

As though suddenly provoked by their vain efforts and the thought that after all their long planning and the killing of the mail clerk and brakeman, they were going to be leaving empty-handed, one of the men glared at fireman Marvin Seng, standing by the engine in his striped cap, nervously holding his gloved hands in the air, and cold-bloodedly shot him with the .45 automatic.

With the realization there were now three dead men and no possibility of obtaining any valuables, one of the bandits yelled at the youngest, still guarding the slender, middle-aged engineer, peering horror-struck from the left side of the cab, "Bump him off and come on." A shot rang out and the engineer crumpled from a gaping hole in the back of the head. There was no longer any question of it being a joking situation; Sid Bates lay limp in his cab, his glasses still in place but his eyes no longer seeing, his gloved hands no longer able to pull the cord on the mournful whistle which had thrilled the thousands of youngsters along his route.

Within a few minutes, the three men disappeared into the nearby wooded mountains, leaving behind them four men dead or dying, 20 sacks and 150 pieces of registered mail in some degree of destruction, numerous passengers with cuts and injuries from flying glass, a smoking and dustfilled tunnel . . . and that was merely the first terrible installment of a fantastic saga in the annals of crime and man-hunting. The steam hissed menacingly and the clanging bell of the engine reverberated through the mountain stillness, sounding a macabre knell for the slain men and the future of the young killers.

Chapter 2

Four Men are Slain

Upon returning to the passenger cars, conductor Marrett obtained flashlights and, after advising the passengers of the supposed boiler explosion, asked for volunteers to return with him to provide first aid assistance. Among those who joined him was Lawrence E. C. Joers, a young medical student, on his way to California.

Stumbling single-file along the narrow, murky space between the train and the tunnel wall, they finally reached the mail car but encountered such an impassible sheet of hissing hot steam that they were forced back, though through the steam they could dimly see the movements of several men, assumed to be the train crew. However, the noise prevented them from hearing anything being said. Backing up, they stooped and crawled under the train, crossing the tracks to the left side of the tunnel, again proceeding toward the engine outside the exit.

On reaching daylight and the engine, no movement was seen, but they did see the hatless engineer slumped over in the cab, dead or unconscious, his train bell still tolling a veritable death dirge. Fireman Seng and the dead-heading brakeman, "Coyl" Johnson, were sprawled on the ground to the right of the engine. Marrett ran as fast as he could to the emergency phone, some 150 yards down the track, and reported the accident, still believing, at that point, an exploding engine had caused all the damage. Medical assistance was urgently requested, as well as a work unit to pull the disabled train from the tunnel before the arrival of the second train section or the work train which was on the west side of the mountain waiting for #13 to pass.

Returning to the engine, Marrett was joined by Herbert Micander, another railroad employee. They removed Bates from the cab and laid him on the ground near Seng and Johnson. Meanwhile, it appeared to the young medical student that Johnson was trying to say something and, thinking he had been overcome by gas or concussion, started to provide artificial respiration. To his object consternation, blood spurted from the body. Upon tearing open the man's clothing, he discovered numerous puncture wounds.

It began to dawn on the young volunteer medic that these were bullet wounds and it was no boiler explosion they were contending with. Quickly he examined Bates and determined he had been shot through the head. Turning to the third body, it was soon ascertained that he, too, had been shot.

During this moving around, Joers tripped over some wires leading up the side of the embankment and, following them, discovered a detonating device. Alongside, in some wrapping paper, was a pair of worn, stained, bib-overalls.

The conductor refused to believe Joer's breathless conclusion that all three victims had been shot and this had been a hold up attempt, until he was led to the detonating machine to see for himself. Whereupon he made another dash for the nearby telephone, to report this stunning new development.

Greatly worried about the mail clerk in the explosion-ripped car, upon his return the conductor asked Joers if he would enter and check on the clerk. Marrett boosted the young man into the open end of the mail car and handed him a flashlight. Having been told the clerk's name was Dougherty, Joers loudly called several times but received no answer. The smoky interior was barely penetrated by the flashlight but he could see everything was in absolute shambles, with many parts still burning. Gingerly poking the flashlight ahead of him, he tried to examine things but the weak beam only revealed burning mail sacks, scattered mail and debris through the smoke and steam seething up from various areas within the car. Choking and coughing, he blindly stumbled around, gradually becoming aware he was getting all "gooed up" with something, and when a cold, wet, object slapped up against his face, he shoved the flashlight at it. To his horror, he discovered it to be a long piece of human flesh and hair, gruesomely dangling from a broken overhead beam.

About this time he stepped on something which felt like a human head and, turning the flashlight downward, was sickened to find the bloody torso and scorched head of a man lying there, eyes closed and the spinal column stripped bare of flesh. The only clothing left on the remains was the collar. Staggering from the car, he blurted his grisly finding to the conductor. It is highly doubtful if, during the balance of his long medical career, his presence of mind and personal self-control were ever again so fully tested.

Mass confusion is always rampant under such unexpected circumstances, with people stumbling over important pieces of evidence: empty shotgun shells . . . empty .45 cartridge cases . . . the detonater . . . overalls . . . wires . . . the dropped .45 at the east entrance, and so on.

The railroad men, true to their long training, were striving to get the damaged train out of the tunnel and the track cleared as quickly as possible, so later units would not be delayed. The injured

Southern Pacific trainmen moved the ruptured express car from the tunnel as quickly as possible so other traffic could pass, and to await detailed investigation by authorities.

passengers were being given first aid prior to returning to Ashland for treatment and the uninjured were being reassured that there was no further danger as the slayers had fled the scene.

While various law enforcement agencies had been rapidly alerted about the attempted train robbery and the accompanying deaths, Sheriff Andrew S. Calkins of Siskiyou County (California) was the first law officer to reach the site. However, in short order several police departments and self-proclaimed posses were resolutely, sometimes even ludicrously, making every effort to prevent the escape of the murderers. Airplanes were called out from the airport in nearby Medford, and these flew low over the mountains, looking for something, although they didn't know just what. There were many of these hastily formed citizen groups roaming around the mountainsides and it was nothing short of a miracle that some of the members didn't shoot each other.

H. G. McCarty, Ashland trainmaster for Southern Pacific, had been temporarily operating from nearby Hornbrook, California, a few miles to the south, and rushed to the site, arriving about 2 p.m., a little more than an hour after the crime began. Realizing the importance of preserving all clues being found scattered around the area, he picked up the detonator (which, of course, had been seen

The interior of the express car was thoroughly devastated by the great force of the blast and the fire which followed.

by numerous people in the meantime, as the copper wires conspicuously led from the wrecked mail car to its nearby location), the overalls, and the accompanying piece of wrapping paper, along with some empty shell casings. These were turned over to W. G. Chandler, special agent for S.P., who arrived at the west portal a short while later. Chandler also picked up several .45 calibre shell casings at the tunnel, along with other evidence, and later noted the shot-up trees which were subsequently identified as having been used for target practice in the vicinity of the murderers' camp.

Chief Special Agent Dan O'Connell had the damaged express car moved to Ashland where it was examined for additional clues.

Almost within minutes of the initial robbery report, Daniel O'Connell, chief of the Southern Pacific agents, had been notified at his office in San Francisco. He left at once, taking with him three of his most able assistants, Dennis Quillinan, Charles Meyers and Ray Guilfoyle. They arrived at the robbery site the following day (October 12th) to lead the investigation. The 56-year-old O'Connell had been credited with the capture of the famed train robber Roy Gardner who, ironically, was one of the idols of the three DeAutremont brothers.

Impetus for a quick solution of the crime was given on Saturday, October 13, when a black-draped funeral train carried the bodies of engineer Bates and fireman Seng, from Ashland south through tunnel # 13 on their way to Dunsmuir for buriel. The following day Reverend J. S. Chaney gave a funeral eulogy in Ashland's Methodist church for the closed-casket remains of Elvyn Dougherty; Coyl Johnson was buried the same day at the IOOF cemetery in Medford. Johnson had been slain one day short of his 38th birthday; his wife Ruby had a party planned for the occasion, upon his return.

O'Connell set up headquarters in Ashland but the slayers appeared to have vanished into thin air and, while clues turned up all over the place, none provided any identity to the wanted men. Southern Pacific special agents Thomas Commer and Patrick

Top: Numerous items of evidence were gathered in the vicinity of the crime. The wooden chest was partially burned in an effort to destroy it but an express tag found in the ashes helped identify the criminals.

Center: Creosote-soaked foot pads and discarded knapsacks were found near the west portal of the tunnel.

Bottom: The detonating machine used to explode the dynamite was discovered in the brush nearby.

Top: S. P. section hands working at the west portal of the tunnel where the crime took place.

Bottom: Much of the mail in the express car was badly burned but the Post Office Department made every possible effort to deliver it and to explain the reason for the damage.

Sweeney found an empty one-pound can of Carnation pepper about 20 feet from the detonating device, along with insulated cap wire. Section foreman Carl Bonderson found wire along the tracks, a reel, 3 knapsacks and creosote-soaked footpads, and was also aware of the nearby overalls and detonator. Brakeman J. H. Benjamin found the .45 Colt automatic pistol, apparently dropped by one of the bandits when climbing aboard the train at the east portal. He also noticed that the serial numbers had been partially filed off.

It was soon ascertained that this abandoned cabin had been occupied by the criminals shortly before the holdup. Note the No Trespassing signs.

S.P. special investigators Vincent L. Arcega and F. E. Ramirez, from Sacramento, California, arrived on the morning of the 12th and began methodically making a scientifically detailed search for evidence. Within a half hour of their arrival they were searching an old cabin on nearby Mt. Crest, which had, obviously, been lived in recently and where a host of interesting items were located. In the ashpan of the stove was an exploded .45 cartridge case, 2 pieces of copper wire, a burned ramrod for a pistol and 2 dry-cell battery carbons. On the cabin porch were gunny sack fragments and a baking pan with creosote in the bottom.

The interior of the cabin occupied by the brothers while planning the crime.

Inside the cabin were various supplies, which indicated someone had been there within the previous few days. Near the semaphore, at the west end of the tunnel, a black grip was found, in which were nine .45 calibre cartridges, a spool of thread and, inside the lining, a needle.

Day after day the Southern Pacific men, local posses, law enforcement people, and ten members of the Oregon National Guard under the command of Captain J. O. Baker criss-crossed the countryside, in search of additional information. Everyone wondered how the fugitives had managed to escape the tight dragnet, and residents for miles around carefully locked their doors and piled furniture high against them at night, for fear the murderers might break in and slay them. Mothers put 'the fear of God' into misbehaving young'uns, by telling them the train robbers would 'get them if they weren't good.'

On October 14th, 22-year-old ex-convict Allen A. Hodges, who had been arrested as a suspect, after Signalman B. R. Arne and his assistant reported having seen him in the vicinity of the tunnel the day prior to the crime, proved he had been in Marshfield the day of the holdup and was released.

Southern Pacific Company
(PACIFIC SYSTEM)

REWARD

This Company will, as to each person who participated in the hold-up of our Train No. 13, at Tunnel 13 near Siskiyou, Jackson County, Oregon, at about 12:40 P. M., Thursday, October 11, 1923, pay a reward of $2500 for information directly leading to arrest and conviction.

Forward information to D. O'Connell, Chief Special Agent, Southern Pacific Company, 65 Market Street, San Francisco, Cal.

J. H. DYER, General Manager.

San Francisco, Oct. 11, 1923.

Within hours of the bloody crime, 2,000 copies of this reward poster had been printed and were being distributed.

De Autremont Brothers

OFFICE OF THE CHIEF INSPECTOR,
Washington, D. C., May 25, 1926.

To all Postmasters
and Postal Employees—

On October 11, 1923, a Southern Pacific passenger train was held up at Siskiyou, Oreg. The mail car was dynamited. A railway postal clerk was killed and his body burned. The engineer, fireman, and brakeman on the train were also murdered.

Three brothers, Roy, Ray, and Hugh De Autremont, are under indictment, charged with the crime, but have not yet been arrested. A reward circular covering the matter is being distributed to those in the Postal Service and through other channels.

It is desired that all postmasters and others receiving the circular give it the widest publicity and make every effort to bring its contents to the attention of the public generally.

RUSH D. SIMMONS,
Chief Inspector.

Special instructions were regularly given to all postal employees to emphasize efforts to capture the fugitives.

Left: Chief Postal Inspector Charles Riddiford, headquartered at Spokane, Washington was in charge of the Post Office's efforts to apprehend those responsible for the terrible crime.

Right: The tenacious Dan O'Connell, Chief Special Agent for the Southern Pacific Company.

A Rulie Johnson had escaped from the Linn County jail in Albany, Oregon, on July 1st. Sheriff Frank Richard of Albany had a poster printed offering $500 reward for Johnson's capture, pointing out that Johnson was a prime suspect in the train holdup.

As late as October 17th, 6 days after the robbery, the indefatigable Mr. Arcega, in the company of Victor Dale and a Mr. Moore, found 2 canteens near the Mt. Crest cabin, which had been overlooked in previous searches.

On October 19th, the Medford *Clarion* reported an interview with a local clairvoyant, who stated, "Four men had robbed the train of a six figure amount of cash and had then joined the other train passengers without being detected."

Mr. O'Connell and his determined group of investigators combed and re-combed the area for further evidence and, while they accumulated a vast number of clues, there was still no identity for the criminals. Although the creosote-dipped, burlap shoe covers and scattered pepper prevented bloodhounds from picking up any trace of scent, through their experienced analysis of the evidence and interview with Hugh Haffey, O'Connell and Chief Postal Inspector Charles Riddiford from Spokane, Washington ascertained that, most likely, there were three men involved in the actual commission of the crime.

Baffled for an immediate path to pursue, O'Connell bundled up the overalls, the found .45 Colt automatic, the three knapsacks, shoe covers and other clues, and instructed Special Agent Ramirez to take them to famed Professor Edward Oscar Heinrich, at the University of California, in Berkeley, California. Heinrich was a Professor of chemistry but also one of the outstanding criminologists of the 20th Century and far-famed for an uncanny capacity to assist police with scientific analysis of evidence; he was often referred to as the "Edison of crime detection" and "Wizard of Berkeley."

Professor Heinrich promised to examine the material at once in his laboratory, first the overalls and knapsacks, for their immediacy, and later the pistol and other material. He advised that he would contact them very shortly with any information uncovered. Perhaps if Professor Heinrich had known that there would be a hassle in getting paid for his work he might have been less diligent or anxious to work with them.

Southern Pacific Company
San Francisco, California

April 7th, 1924.

Mr. C.E. Terrill,
Sheriff, Jackson County,
Jacksonville, Oregon.

My dear Mr. Terrill:

Referring to examination of exhibits and finding of valuable evidence on same by Professor Heinrich, which was sent to him after conference with the District Attorney, yourself and the other officers, Heinrich's bill being $666.90, all of which the County, as you know, was responsible for.

Last week the Commissioners allowed half of this bill, and needless to say, the Professor will be greatly disappointed. I know that you will consider this a reasonable bill, as when the question of Professor Mays was brought up, you will recall you stated that Mays had charged $1100.00 or $1300.00 on a single murder case he worked on. Will you kindly take this up with the Commissioners and Judge Gardner and have the remaining part of the bill put through.

The Southern Pacific Company is still spending money following up clues, but being that they do not materialize into anything important, we have not been burdening your files by writing you on them, but you may be assured when the DeAutremont brothers are located you will be promptly notified.

Hoping you are in your usual good health, I am

Yours very truly,

D. O'Connell

DO'C/Q

Chapter 3

Professor Heinrich's Evidence

Within a few days, a flood of information began pouring from Professor Heinrich's laboratory. One of the men they were seeking was a left-handed, brown-haired, white man, about 5 feet 10 inches tall, weighing about 165 pounds. He would be around 21 to 25 years of age, was probably quite fastidious in his personal habits, and most likely had recently been working as a lumberjack in Western Oregon.

O'Connell and Riddiford were incredulous; local authorities ridiculed the findings—lumberjacks didn't try to rob trains. The professor carefully explained the reasons for his deductions. He had taken the overalls found at the scene of the crime and thoroughly examined them, inch by inch, thread by thread. Measuring the overalls from cuff to waist, he compared the worn spots with similar clothing, enabling him to establish the height of the suspect. The waist size and height enabled him to make a reasonably accurate estimate of the weight. (The professor did slightly overestimate the weight, by some 25 pounds, and the height by 5 inches.)

Two hairs had been found, caught on the overalls, which, upon microscopic examination, gave him information. Hair has a tendency to lose its pigmentation and other characteristics in direct proportion to the age of the person growing it, enabling an experienced scientist, such as Heinrich, to make an educated guess as to the correct age.

What had initially appeared to be grease stains on the overalls, upon analysis turned out to be pitch from the Douglas Fir, most commonly found in the lumbering areas of western Oregon. To further substantiate this theory, the discerning professor also found tiny fragments of Douglas Fir needles in the pockets.

In the right hand pocket and in the right pants cuff, small Douglas Fir chips were found. As Heinrich pointed out, a left-handed person stands with his right side closest to a tree while chopping and chips would have a tendency to lodge on the nearest side of the clothing; therefore, most likely, one of the suspects would be left-handed—the one owning the overalls. (Again he was in error in that none of the holdup men was left handed.)

Professor Edward Oscar Heinrich, University of California at Berkeley, was far-famed for his scientific criminology techniques and often called the "Wizard of Berkeley" or "Edison of Crime Detection."

The professor had used a small vacuum cleaner device, with which he further cleaned the overalls and separated the various bits of material thereby obtained. Among the identifiable items were filings from human fingernails, and he stated, "a man who carries a fingernail file is usually fastidious, not only so far as his nails are concerned but about his general appearance."

This mass of logic overwhelmed the investigators, but, to add even more to the mountain of information unearthed, Heinrich handed them a piece of very specific evidence—a small wrinkled, rectangular piece of paper, perhaps an inch and a half by two and a half inches. It was postal receipt #236-L, for a registered letter, dated Sept. 14, 1923, sent from Eugene, Oregon. The probing professor had found it wadded into a tiny ball and shoved to the bottom of the pencil pocket in the overalls.

The authorities rushed to check out the receipt and found it had been issued to a Roy DeAutremont and sent to a Verne DeAutremont in Lakewood, New Mexico. Quickly they checked on Roy DeAutremont and, to their absolute astonishment, discovered him to be a brown-haired, 23-year old lumberjack, who had recently quit his job at the Silver Falls Lumber Co., in Silverton, Oregon, where he had been employed with his twin brother, Ray. In addition, he had been a barber and was known for his personal neatness and continual filing of his fingernails.

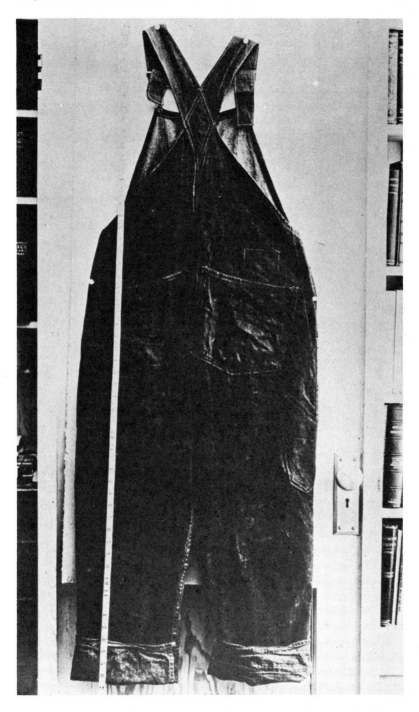

This pair of overalls were discarded at the scene of the crime and provided a fountain of clues through the efforts of Professor Heinrich.

RECEIPT FOR REGISTERED ARTICLE   No. _____

Registered at the Post Office Indicated in Postmark   *Class postage* _____

Complete record of registered mail is kept
at the post office, but the sender should write
the name of the addressee on back hereof as
an identification.   Preserve and submit this
receipt in case of inquiry.

POSTMASTER,

Postmark clearly,
showing
date and office.

Form 3806.   Per_____   05—6882

This receipt for registered mail, discovered by Professor Heinrich in the pocket of
the overalls quickly identified one of the suspects.

Upon interviewing the father of the suspect, Paul DeAutremont,
a barber in Eugene, Oregon, it was learned he was greatly worried
about his three sons, Roy, Ray and Hugh, who had left several
weeks earlier on a hunting trip to the Puget Sound area and had not
returned. He emotionally decried any thought of his boys being involved in the crime, stating, "My boys are good boys; they could not
do a thing like that."

A horde of investigators spread out over the State of Oregon, interviewing everyone they could find who had known any of the three
boys or the family. It was quickly ascertained that Roy and his twin
brother, Ray, were practically inseparable. While there were three
other brothers, 19-year-old Hugh had been with the twins in recent
months and had disappeared along with them from known haunts;
none of the three had been seen for weeks. Detectives descended
upon the DeAutremont home and stripped it of all the three
brothers' possessions, in search of more information or leads as to
where they might be found.

A friend of the hunted men, Bernard LeChance, was arrested
and, while he readily admitted this friendship, he quickly established an alibi, stating as well that he thoroughly doubted their guilt.

To the surprise of the detectives, they also discovered that Ray
was an ex-convict, having, at the age of 20, served a year for
criminal syndicalism in the Washington State Reformatory at
Monroe, from May 25, 1920 to May 12, 1921.

Meanwhile, back in Berkeley, Professor Heinrich was doggedly
busy in his laboratory. On the piece of towel found in the cabin near
the crime scene, he discovered another small piece of human hair,
which, upon examination, proved to have come from the same man
whose hair was on the overalls. On the towel was also a tiny frag-
ment of red wool thread, which he suggested might have come from
a red wool sweater. Among the possessions taken from the DeAutre-

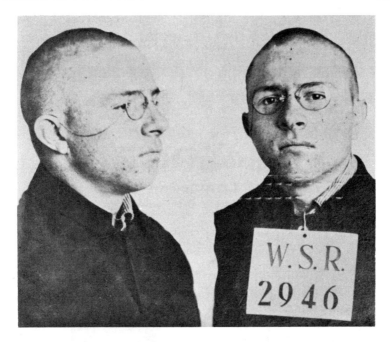

Ray DeAutremont, in 1920, as prisoner #2946 at the Washington State Reformatory where he served a sentence for Criminal Syndicalism.

mont home was a red sweater, belonging to Ray and the tiny thread matched its texture perfectly.

The accumulating mass of evidence provided by the amazing professor, along with what the detectives were digging up in Oregon, was weaving a tighter and tighter web around the three. But, where were they? They had completely disappeared. Rumors swiftly circulated around Ashland and Medford that someone was concealing the killers . . . that there would likely be more killings before it was all over . . . that there was a lot more to the crime than met the eye. The fact that the body of the poor mail clerk, practically disintegrated in the blast, was not shown at the time of burial, created some extremely vicious speculation that he was in on the crime and had fled to Europe or somewhere with the loot, where he would be joined later by the murderers. In fact, this totally baseless gossip cruelly pursued his hapless widow for years. The facts are that she was left with a mortgage payment, a 4-year-old son, and $3,000 in insurance. Eventually, she did receive $35 a month pension with $10 a month for her son.

Posses continued to prowl the rugged mountains in search of the missing suspects. While most of the rumors were merely figments of someone's twisted imagination, they did provide hot fuel for an already badly overheated and confused situation.

One of the knapsacks discovered at the site was found to have

Train Holdup of S.P. Co. Train No. 1-13, Siskiyou, Oregon, October 11, 1923. Four Men Killed.

REWARD
of $4800.00
For Arrest and Conviction of Each Man

At least three implicated. Below are photographs and descriptions of two of three brothers wanted in connection with the holdup. Should be arrested on sight and held incommunicado.

Wire information, charges collect, to D. O'Connell, Chief Special Agent, Southern Pacific Railroad Company, or to C. Riddiford, Post Office Inspector in Charge, Ashland, Oregon, or to C. E. Terrill, Sheriff, Jackson County, at Medford, Oregon.

No. 1. Roy DeAutremont

Age: 23 years
Weight: 135 to 140 lbs.
Hair: Medium light, bleached by sun
Height: 5 ft. 6 inches
Complexion: Sandy
Eyes: Light brown. Small. Wears glasses at times, and eyes appear granulated and squinty.
Face broad, short cut neck, long nose and prominent nostrils
Face smooth. No marks. Head round
Twin brother of Number Two.

No. 2. Ray DeAutremont

Age: 23 years

Height: 5 ft. 6 inches

Weight: 135 to 140 lbs.

Complexion: Sandy

Hair as shown in Number one.

Broad face, short cut neck, face smooth.

Eyes: Light brown and small.

Twin brother of Number One.

No. 3. Hugh DeAutremont, alias E. E. James

Age: 19—Looks older
Height: 5 ft. 7 inches
Weight: 135 lbs.
Complexion: Fair
Eyes: Blue
Nose: Slightly pug

Hair: Medium light, slightly sandy and curly
Smooth shaven, wore short test rain coat; also had mackinaw, but don't know what color
Brother of Numbers One and Two.

No. 4. Barnard LeChance

Age: About 30 years
Height: 5 ft. 8 inches
Weight: 150 lbs.

Hair: Black, large quantity of hair
Small black mustache
Is known as a Radical and Organizer.

Ashland, Oregon, October 21, 1923.

Within a few days of the holdup the suspected criminals had been identified with this reward poster. The pictures of Roy and Ray DeAutremont were glued on the posters by hand.

While the exterior serial numbers were scratched off this .45 Colt Automatic, there was little difficulty in quickly tracing it to the purchaser.

been sewed with a heavy black thread. The overalls had been repaired with a similar black thread. Upon examination, it was ascertained the same type of thread had been used for both, identical to the spool of thread found in the black grip.

The .45 Colt automatic pistol, picked up at the tunnel entrance, with the serial numbers filed off, was assumed to have been dropped by one of the bandits. It was sent to the Colt factory in Hartford, Connecticut, for   detailed examination and report. Removal of the serial numbers by filing only temporarily holds up identification, in that the numbers are stamped into the steel, which permanently disturbs the metal. A chemical treatment can quickly reveal the original numbers. However Colt also has the serial number on the inside of its pistols and when disassembled number 130763 was quickly found. Additionally, the barrel had a separate number, #379208, which was visible upon being removed.

The Colt people were eager to cooperate and shortly advised the weapon had been sold in 1923 to Schwabacker Hardware Co., (a wholesaler), in Seattle, Washington, who in turn, advised it had been shipped to Hauser Brothers, a sporting goods store, in Albany, Oregon. The records of Hauser Brothers showed the gun had subsequently been sold to a William Elliott. Upon comparing the signature with the known signatures of the brothers, obtained from the Silver Falls Lumber Company records, handwriting experts unequivocally agreed that William Elliott and Ray DeAutremont were one and the same.

Piles of evidence were being uncovered by the detectives. Bullets dug from the tree trunks near the Mt. Crest cabin on the Siskiyous and bullets from the stumps at the Silver Falls Lumber Company, where the DeAutremonts were known to have target practiced, were found to have been fired from the same weapons.

Stanley V. Cochrane, of Springfield, Oregon, advised he had sold the brothers 1,000 rounds of ammunition and had personally delivered part of it to them.

At one time, Hugh had apparently voiced an admiration for Jesse James and was known to have spent a night in a hotel with a girl, registered as J. James and wife. Practically every hotel register in western Oregon was checked. Pay dirt was hit in several places, including three locations in Ashland, where, on September 26, 1923, he had stayed at the Fairview Rooming House, on September 27th at the Park Hotel, and on September 28th at the Gurna Rooming House, registering, in each instance, as E. E. James. These signatures each had an oddly formed capital "J" and a small "i" with a circle, instead of a dot, wherever the letter "i" was written.

One of the biggest breaks came at a skid-row hotel in Portland where they spotted the signature of one "J. James", in the same handwriting as the previously found J. James, and unquestionably that of Hugh. Even more conclusive were the two signatures directly above, which were identified as the handwriting of Roy and Ray. It was also ascertained the hotel towels were identical to the one from the Siskiyou cabin, except the hotel name had been torn off the towel found at the cabin.

Sometimes the intuitive hunch of an investigator pays big dividends. Across the street from the drab hotel was a small department store. Upon checking with them, it was learned the cheap tableware stocked was the same brand as the knives, forks and spoons found at the mountain cabin. Examination of the store records rewarded the investigators with information which showed

A handsome, young Roy DeAutremont could hardly have conceived when he had these pictures taken for a girl friend that later they would stare back at him from a reward poster.

Left: A debonair Ray DeAutremont.

Right: Who could have guessed that the 1923 high school graduation picture of popular Hugh DeAutremont would later appear on reward posters throughout the world.

REWARD!
$14,400.00
Holdup of Southern Pacific Train No. 13, 1st Section, at Siskiyou, October 11, 1923

FOUR MEN KILLED

Reward of $2500.00 will be paid by the Southern Pacific Railroad Company, of $300.00 by the American Railway Express Company, and not to exceed $2,000.00 by the United States, for the arrest and conviction of each person implicated in the holdup.

At least three persons participated in the crime. Below are photographs and descriptions of three brothers who are believed to have been connected with the holdup and who should be arrested on sight and held incommunicado.

DESCRIPTIONS

No. 1. Ray DeAutremont—Age 23 years; weight 135 to 140 lbs.; hair medium light brown; height 5 feet 6 inches; complexion medium light; eyes light brown, rather small; wears nose eye glasses to read with; eyes appear somewhat granulated and squinty; face broad, short cut neck, long nose and prominent nostrils. Face smooth. No marks. Head round.

No. 2. Ray DeAutremont—Age 23 years; height 5 feet 6 inches; weight 135 to 140 lbs.; complexion, medium light; hair, medium light brown; broad face; prominent nostrils; short cut neck; face smooth; eyes, light brown and small. Eye tooth right side gold crown. Finger Print Classification:

31   1MM   14.
28   9II   17.

Sentenced to one year Monroe, Washington, Reformatory, November 17th, 1919. I. W. W. Organizer. Wears glasses when reading.

No. 3. Hugh DeAutremont—Age 19, looks older. Height 5 feet 7 inches; weight 135 lbs.; complexion fair; eyes blue; nose, slightly pug; hair medium light, slightly sandy and curly, bleached by the sun; smooth shaven; wore short test rain coat; also had Mackinaw, but don't know what color.

The above described men are twin brothers. It is most difficult for those not well acquainted with them to tell them apart. The distinguishing features are that Ray probably weighs three or four pounds more and is a trifle taller than Roy. Ray is also slightly stooped over. Ray is more given to talk and pleasantry than Roy, who is inclined to be quiet and unassuming. They have both learned the barber trade and have worked in the woods as loggers and it is probable that instead of being dressed up they may be dressed roughly and as loggers.

All three men are loggers and may be found in logging camps working as choker setters, hook tenders or whistle punks. They have spoken of taking a long sea voyage and look-out should be kept for them attempting to ship at sea ports. They speak Spanish fluently and may attempt to cross the Mexican border. Formerly lived at Lakewood, New Mexico.

Photographs of Roy and Hugh were taken about a year ago; of Ray, taken in 1920.

Wire information, charges collect, to D. O'Connell, Chief Special Agent, Southern Pacific Railroad Company, Ashland, Oregon; C. E. Terrill, Sheriff, Jackson County, Jacksonville, Oregon, or C. Riddiford, Post Office Inspector in Charge, Spokane, Wash.

Postmasters will post and publish and distribute to Rural and Star Route Carriers, also see to it that all Peace Officers are supplied with these circulars.

C. RIDDIFORD,   D. O'CONNELL,
Post Office Inspector in Charge,   Chief Special Agent, Southern Pacific R. R. Company, Ashland, Oregon
Spokane, Washington

Case No. 57883-D   Ashland, Oregon, October 24, 1923.

Seattle PO—11-13-23—40M

40,000 copies of poster #5 were printed on November 13, 1923 at a cost of $60.

delivery of identical tableware to a Mr. J. James, at the hotel across the street, while he was registered there.

All three of the DeAutremont brothers had now been definitely linked to the scene of the crime—Roy through his hair on the overalls and towel, Ray through his purchase of the gun found at the scene, and now Hugh through his buying of the tableware. The web of evidence was conclusive. But where were the three fugitives? Not a single verified sighting had been made since the crime and, apparently, they had vanished from the face of the earth.

Major crimes always present a multitude of hoaxes, wild-eyed clues and stories which, upon investigation, turn out to be totally false. The publicity and circumstances surrounding this case brought more than its warranted share. For example, on November 3rd, Sheriff W. B. Mercer and two deputies of Goldfield, Nevada, reported they had trailed the DeAutremonts in a car to a remote ranch; the suspects had been found eating breakfast but had escaped, leaving their car behind. On that same date, William Hard and Robert (French) Erno were believed to have slain Fred Skeen, a Siskiyou County rancher, to prevent him from divulging information relative to the holdup.

ENTHUSIASTIC OFFERS OF ASSISTANCE VIRTUALLY INUNDATED THE AUTHORITIES.

November 24th, 1923.

Mr. C. E. Terrill, Sheriff,
  Jacksonville, Oregon.

Dear sir:-

I just received a notice of reward offered for Roy, Ray and Hugh DeAutremont, who are wanted in your County, in connection with the holding up of a Southern Pacific Train and killing four men.

I am sure that the above three men passed through this town about the last of October or the first of November. They stopped at a small restruant (sic) to get something to eat about 11 o'clock one morning.

I was in the restruant (sic) at the time and looked them over good. One of them wore nose glasses and he also did most of the talking.

They were rather roughly dressed and had not shaved in some time.

They claimed to be traveling men and had come from Arizona and were going to Forth Worth, Texas.

They were in a Ford Touring Car which was in rather bad shape.

I examined their car to see what they had, but did not see anything except an old suit case, a part of a box of apples and two or three old quilts.

I went back the second time and looked them over, and they appeared to be somewhat nervous and watched me very closely, most especially the youngest of the three.

One of my Deputies lived as neighbor to these three men near Lakewood, New Mexico, and has known them for several years, and is well acquainted with them, however he was not in town at the time they passed through.

If I can be of any service to you in locating the above men I will be glad to assist you.

Yours very truly

J.C. Keller
Sheriff, Yoakum County, Texas.

Plains, Texas.

It was astonishing to the authorities how the fugitives could have made so many absolutely stupid mistakes prior to the crime and yet be so clever in avoiding the vast forces so diligently searching for them.

In any event, the officials felt their case was strong enough for prosecution and, on November 23, 1923, six indictments were issued at Jacksonville, Oregon, charging the trio:

627-C First degree murder of Marvin Seng.
628-C First degree murder of Elvyn Earl Dougherty.
629-C First degree murder of Charles Orin Johnson.
630-C First degree murder of Sidney Lloyd Bates.
631-C Attempt to burglarize a Southern Pacific mail car.
632-C Stopping a train with intent to commit larceny.

It was later discovered that there was no Federal Statute covering the crime of murdering a postal employee, so the charge was changed to assault with intent to commit larceny, under Section #197, and in U. S. District Court for the District of Oregon, on Dec. 17, 1923, a Grand Jury returned an indictment for violation of the Penal Code (Docket #C-10488), charging the three missing men with assaulting Elvyn Dougherty, the slain mail clerk, in their attempt to commit larceny, and, in the execution thereof, with murdering the mail clerk.

Chapter 4

Search for the Murderers

S.P.'s Dan O'Connell and Post Office Inspector Charles Rid-diford well realized the pressures to solve the spectacularly brutal crime. With the huge number of clues, plus an established identity of at least some of the criminals involved, they felt quite confident of a quick solution. However, as the weeks passed and months turned into years, they lost much of their optimism. Nevertheless, they carefully checked out each report, no matter how ludicrous or far-fetched it appeared.

Being thoroughly professional detectives and fully aware that much police work is pure dogged routine, they began this routine almost immediately. Inquiries had been made to various law enforcement officials throughout the northwest in conjunction with mailing the first reward posters, prior to the identification of the DeAutremonts. Some of the returns received made interesting reading:

Seattle, Wash. October 15, 1923
General Agent, SP RR
Seattle, Wash.

Dear Sir:

Regarding holdup of train No. 13 at Siskiyou. After an exhaustive investigation of probable suspects that may be connected in this case, I take pleasure in submitting to you the following names, together with their records, that I have obtained from the authorities at the Walla Walla Penitentiary, to wit:

Al Meadors, and X out of Salem, Oregon, who served time for train robbery. Has only been at liberty a few months. This man is utterly fearless and was a partner of "Dutch" Frank Wagner, one of the best box men west of the Mississippi River.

Bill Robinson, also an X out of Salem. This man is a pal of Meadors and knows the Siskiyou's like a book. Is considered a dangerous man and quick on the draw. Has been convicted of horse stealing and at one time stood off a posse in south western Oregon successfully.

"Blackie" McDade, also an X out of Salem. This man received a 12 year sentence at Jacksonville, Jackson County, Oregon, for a stick up of a freight train in the Siskiyou's either in the latter part of 1920 or 1921. Feels very bitter against the railroad men of the

Siskiyou Division for testifying against him. Formerly a railroad fireman and a bad man.

From the information I gather the manner and style of the holdup seem to correspond with the actions and activities of these men in the past and if they happened to be any where in this vicinity lately no doubt they are the men connected with this deal. Would suggest that you obtain pictures of them from Salem, or if you would rather I will be glad to get them for you.

Trusting that the above information will be of service to you, I am,

Very truly yours.

Matt Starwich, Sheriff.

Seattle, Wash., Oct. 17th, 1923
M. Coturri, Esq.
Special Agent SP - Portland, Ore.
Daniel O'Connell
Special Agent SP - San Francisco

Dear Sirs:

Regarding holdup of train 13 - Siskiyou.

Since writing you on the 15th inst regarding the above holdup I have obtained the following added information from the Penitentiary authorities at Walla Walla which I think is worthy of consideration.

"Blackie" McDade. Was convicted and sentenced to 12 years for a stickup of an SP crew on the "Hump" between Ashland and Dunsmuir. It was the evidence of the railroad men that convicted him, and I happen to know that he would jump at a chance to bump off a few of them if the opportunity offered. Formerly a railroad fireman and brakeman, he is entirely familiar with details necessary to pull a stunt like the last one. During his short confinement in Salem he became closely associated with Meadors, Robinson, Jenkins and through sources of information that I have, I know that their daily conversation was regarding ways and means to make a money train upon their release from Salem. There seems to be plenty of foundation for a suspicion in this man's case and for the death of the train crew, which seems on the face to be an unnecessary act, this man would through his hatred of the division crews, have a motive.

"Bill" Robinson, formerly a cow and sheep man for Bill Brown over in Lake County, Oregon. This man knows every inch of the hills and mountains from Lakeview clear through to Bend, Oregon. He has stolen horses and sheep for Brown all over Eastern and Southern Oregon. Meadors and Robinson were inseparable and are still, up to the last information I had regarding them. Robinson has a cabin in the foot hills some where over around the mountains between Bend and Lakeview. Also has a camp in the mountains, back of Klamath that is practically inaccessible except to those that know the country. He is a good all round horseman and excellent shot with rifle and pistol. Has a grudge against every body in general because of his two jolts in Salem.

"Meadors" was a partner of Manning and Stoner. They stuck up an O.W. train in Eastern Oregon. Manning was shot dead during the holdup. Meadors was the leader. They were captured and convicted. Meadors, after serving about five years of the sentence was given a conditional pardon and immediately hooked up with Frank Wagner, "Box man". He was in on the Astoria robbery that Wagner pulled and through a woman of Wagner's they were captured in St. Joe, Mo., and brought back to Astoria for trial. Meadors was returned to Salem to finish the balance of his sentence, while Wagner was tried in two courts and given sentences aggregating 40 years. Wagner was shot and killed in a shack outside of Astoria after escaping from Salem.

From my informant I understand that Meadors stands pretty well with certain officers in and around Portland and has been shown some favors by them, hence it might be well to keep any inquiries regarding him under cover. He is supposed to be a clever fellow and seems to have a desire to make a money train at some time or other. He has acquired considerable information regarding railroad shipments of money, location etc. has plenty of nerve and can use a gun when necessary. I also understand that he carries a grudge against special agents Hunter and Woods, and if the opportunity presented itself he would be more than apt to get even with them.

Regarding the appearance of the Hodge brothers, and their having been seen in the hills around Siskiyou, I understand that they either had or have a homestead somewhere in Southern Oregon, and they are supposed to be continually in the woods either hunting or trapping, and are not overburdened with intelligence. The whole family, as I understand it, are feeble minded to a degree and do not seem to possess the nerve necessary to pull a job of this kind.

Trusting that the above information will be of added benefit to you, and assuring you of my co-operation at all times, I beg to remain,

Very truly yours,

Matt Starwich
Sheriff

Unfortunately, in this instance, none of the information helped the case, nor did the many similar letters.

While reward notices providing superficial details of the holdup had been rushed into distribution within hours of the crime, even though names of any suspects were unknown, it was not even certain how many people had been involved. However, by October 22nd the suspects were tentatively identified and posters with pictures and detailed information about them were hurried to all corners of the country, offering substantial rewards for their capture and conviction. The third poster-printing contained pictures of the twins, each of which had to be hand-pasted on the individual poster, together with the name and description of Hugh DeAutre-

Kindly Post in a Conspicuous Place

United States of America
POST OFFICE DEPARTMENT

$15,900 REWARD IN GOLD!

$5,300 Reward For Each Man!

ON OCTOBER 11, 1923, A SOUTHERN PACIFIC RAILWAY TRAIN WAS BLOWN UP NEAR SISKIYOU, OREGON, U. S. A. THE MAIL CLERK WAS KILLED AND HIS BODY BURNED, AND THREE TRAINMEN WERE SHOT AND KILLED. CONCLUSIVE EVIDENCE OBTAINED SHOWS THAT ROY, RAY AND HUGH DE AUTREMONT, THREE BROTHERS, WHO LIVED IN EUGENE, OREGON, COMMITTED THE CRIME. THEIR PHOTOGRAPHS AND GENERAL DESCRIPTIONS ARE SHOWN ON THIS POSTER.

Help in locating the criminals who committed this terrible crime.

REWARDS TOTALING $15,900 WILL BE PAID FOR INFORMATION LEADING TO THE ARREST AND CONVICTION OF THESE MEN. THE UNITED STATES OFFICERS HAVE CONCLUSIVE EVIDENCE AND WILL TAKE CARE OF THE PROSECUTION.

ANY INFORMATION CONCERNING THE WHEREABOUTS OF THESE MEN SHOULD BE COMMUNICATED IMMEDIATELY TO THE NEAREST POLICE OFFICER. IF CONVINCED THE SUSPECTS ARE THE MEN WANTED, NOTIFY THE PERSONS NAMED BELOW BY WIRE.

SIGNATURES OF THE MEN:

$15,900.00 REWARD IN GOLD

Train Hold-up and Murder

$15,900.00 Reward in Gold!

$15,900.00 REWARD!

UNITED STATES
Post Office Department

Train Hold-up and Murder

$15,900.00 Reward in Gold!

More than 2½ million reward posters were printed and distributed throughout the world. 260,000 copies of poster #13 were printed on July 23, 1926 at a cost of $670.90.

mont and Bernard LeChance. LeChance was a friend of the DeAutremonts but quickly proved his non-involvement in the crime.

The Southern Pacific offered $2,500 for each of the killers; American Express offered $300 and the U.S. Government offered $2,000 . . . a total of $14,400 for the three. In addition, several rewards were offered from other sources, most of which were withdrawn before the fugitives were captured. Eventually, a total of 2,265,000 circulars were printed and distributed throughout the world, including 180,000 in Spanish, 40,000 in French, 25,000 in Portuguese, 10,000 in German and 10,000 in Dutch.

Supplementing the wanted men's photos, detailed descriptions were given, right down to the turned-up toe nail of Ray and a listing of their known habits. Data was even provided on the watches carried by them when last known.

There was a multitude of extremely fanciful theories as to who had committed the bloody crime, and how, with some people even suggesting the three missing young men had been slain by hardened criminals who had actually held up the train and committed the murders. However, O'Connell and Riddiford were thoroughly convinced the three DeAutremonts were solely responsible and launched a man hunt lasting for more than three years and eventually cost

VERZOEKE DIT BILJET OP EENE IN HET OOG VALLENDE PLAATS AAN TE PLAKKEN! DEZEN KANT BOVEN, A. U. B.

$15,900 BELOONING IN GOUD!

$5,300 BELOONING UITGELOOFD VOOR IEDEREN MAN!

ROY A. A. DE AUTREMONT

RAY CHARLES DE AUTREMONT

HUGH DE AUTREMONT

HANDTEEKENINGEN VAN DE DADERS

$15,900 BELOONING IN GOUD!

$15,900 BELOONING

VEREENIGDE STATEN VAN AMERIKA
ADMINISTRATIE DER POSTERIJEN

Treinberooving en Moord

VAN

drie spoorwegbeambten en een postbode in de Siskiyou bergen in den Staat Oregon

POSTWAGEN NA BEROOVING

$15,900 BELOONING IN GOUD!

RECOMPENSA de 15,900 DÓLARES ORO

$5,300 RECOMPENSA POR CADA HOMBRE

ROY A. A. DE AUTREMONT

RAY CHARLES DE AUTREMONT

HUGH DE AUTREMONT

FIRMAS DE LOS DELINCUENTES

RECOMPENSA DE $15,900
Oro Americano

Asalto Armado de un Tren y Asesinato

RECOMPENSA DE $15,900
Oro Americano

RECOMPENSA LA SUMA DE $15,9
Oro Americano

DIRECCIÓN GENERAL DE CORREOS
ESTADOS UNIDOS DE NORTE AMÉRICA

Asalto Armado de un Tren y Asesinato
Tres Empleados y un Agente Postal en las Montañas de Siskiyou, Estado de Oregon

RECOMPENSA DE $15,9
Oro Americano

Reward posters were printed in English, French, Spanish, Dutch, German and Portuguese.

well over $500,000. (A great deal of money in the 1920's.

In view of the fugitives' ability to speak fluent Spanish, particular attention was given to Mexico, with the Border Patrol being instructed to examine everyone crossing very carefully. One S.P. special agent, following a tip, went to Mexico with a Post Office inspector, but when rampaging rebel armies were encountered, they both quickly turned back, not being that anxious to trace down the lead.

Postal inspectors visited Mexico City and personally requested the assistance of Mexican postal officials in locating the elusive fugitives. Circulars printed in Spanish were displayed in Post Offices throughout Mexico. Postmasters there were requested to make a survey of all Americans within delivery of their offices.

The persistent Dan O'Connell also arranged to have these circulars displayed in Mexican railroad stations and distributed to Mexican railroad officials.

There were numerous reports of the vanished brothers having been sighted in various parts of Latin America, and Post Office inspectors traveled there extensively in following these leads, but no actual proof could ever be found of the boys' presence there.

Reports poured in to the authorities from all parts of the world. Many over-enthusiastic law-enforcement officers arrested suspects on the slightest pretext. Ironically, it was discovered that many of those arrested were actually wanted on other charges and were sentenced as a result. It was a tough time for wanted men.

All railroad special agents throughout the U. S. were circularized and they, in turn, carefully reconnoitered their train yards, regularly rousting the "bindle stiffs" in nearby hobo "jungles". All barber shops in the U. S. were plastered with posters. All jewelry stores received flyers containing detailed descriptions of the boys' watches. All railroad and bus depots had reward notices prominently posted.

These thousands of posters brought in a continuing barrage of tips and practically every left-handed young man in the country found himself under suspicion at one time or another. Some amateur bounty hunters spent all their spare time covering every nearby sandlot baseball game, looking for anyone throwing left-handed. Others occupied their non-working hours hanging around the bus and train depots, peering at the passengers.

In southern Oregon, W. G. Chandler, the local S. P. special agent, was particularly busy checking out hundreds of local reports—every bootlegger, hard-case, ex-convict, etc. was thoroughly investigated. As Mr. Chandler said, "half the people in southern Oregon who had any enemies were reported to the authorities." A number of persons in California were similarly honored as the following letter indicates:

Mr. D. O'Connell

I notice that they still have the poster out for the men that blew up the car by tunnell (sic) 13, 1923.

I don't see what they are looking for when they have the guilty party right in front of their noses. That is the man that framed up the scheme and leader of the gang. Just go about it the right way. He will explain you all the secret. His name is William Reynolds, and at that time he was employed by the S. P. Co. as a watchman at Dunsmuir.

Very truly yours

The Unknown

Mr. Reynolds was of course, not involved in the crime, other than he, too, had some ideas of who was responsible and on Dec. 3, 1923 passed on several names to Chandler for further investigation. One wonders if "The Unknown" was one of these. Reynolds was not alone in being accused, as many other S.P. employees were the subject of slanderous insinuation and gossip. For many months the purchase of a new car or undue show of prosperity by an S. P. employee in the region brought forth unwarranted suspicions and interrogation.

A close surveillance was maintained on the mail of everyone connected with the DeAutremonts and when A. S. DeAutremont, a cousin of Paul DeAutremont, wrote him a letter of condolence from Los Angeles, the authorities descended in force. Even after learning that he was a relative, a close watch was kept on him for months to see if he was in contact with any of the wanted brothers.

Dorothy Wiberg, Roy's former girl friend, received a letter mailed from Alameda, California, and signed Marion Jobes, which was thought to be an alias for Roy. It set off a flurry of investigation and interrogations of innocent people. (Many of the investigative efforts of that time would today be considered serious violations of the civil rights of the persons involved.)

Alburtus, crystal gazer, traveled the theatre circuit answering questions from the audience and when asked about the DeAutremonts, authoritatively stated, "They are in Buenos Aires and will never be caught." Alexander the Great, also a crystal gazer, capitalized on the crime for some personal publicity and bookings. However, for pure imagination, hypnotist A. E. Gallen, of Portland, had to win a prize, as three police officers reported following their investigation:

Officers Report

Time 9 p.m. .... Portland, Oct. 30th, 1923

Subject: Information.
Chief Jenkins.

About 9:00 p.m. Ins. Schum had a call to Room No. 200,
Princess Hotel, stating he could tell us where the S.P. holdup men
were. He sent officer Nelson and I over. A. E. Gallen rooms at the
above place and he had a young lady that he hypnatize (sic) and
she gave the information. She stated that they were five men in
the job, four of them are now twenty-five miles East of Hood
River, Ore. camped on an old logging road, will hear in morning.
Namely, Thos. Durmont, Blake McFarlane, Larame, and Bert
Harney, the latter two being brothers. She also states that the
other man (Duncan) is near the California line waiting for the
above four men. She said Durmont is the one who did most of the
killing on the job and Larme (sic) Harney is the boy that touched
off the blast that wrecked the car.

Gallen says he will go and show just where the camp is and is
very anxious to do it. She described the dress of the men and said
they were driving a Dodge car with Ore. license stolen off of Ford
car. No. 3458. They may be mistaken, so she told me. Ins. did not
hear her say this as Sergeant Thatcher wants us to come down this
A.M. and see you. Will tell you more if I can think of them.

Schum, Nelson and Williams.

While the officials didn't pursue the investigation in depth, they
did check it out.

Mr. O'Connell received a letter from Thomas R. Colton, of Redding, Calif., advising that he thought he had traveled with Hugh
during Oct. 1923 while "beating their way". The special agent there
reported that Colton had frequently expressed great interest in
becoming a detective. But meanwhile he had skipped town with
another man's wife.

A report was received from Harry McClellan, in Marshfield,
Oregon, that Ray DeAutremont's name was written on the restroom
wall of the Chandler Hotel. Tracings were carefully made and compared with Ray's signature. They were not the same.

People with extremely supple imaginations approached the
authorities with highly plausible stories, each of which had to be
thoroughly investigated. These false leads must have been
thoroughly exasperating and the patience of the detectives tremendously strained. Although none of the perpetrators of false information were prosecuted, the thought surely must have entered the
authorities' minds after the encounter with Lewis G. Bennett.

In Dec. 1923 reports were received that a Mr. Bennett had some
vital information. Special agent M. F. McCarthy was instructed to
follow through. McCarthy eventually was contacted by the attorney
for Mr. Bennett and then proceeded to Las Vegas, Nevada, to con-
fer with Bennett and his attorney:

WESTERN UNION TELEGRAM:

Las Vegas, Nev. 938 A. Jan. 2, 1924

M. F. McCARTHY
SPECIAL AGENT SOUTHERN PACIFIC RY, ARCADE
STATION 2ND FLOOR, LOS ANGELES.

BENNETT WILL MEET YOU HERE MONDAY, JANUARY
SEVENTH. ADVISE IF SATISFACTORY.

E. F. DUPRAY.

Los Angeles, Calif., January 8, 1924
Mr. D. O'Connell:

Referring to subsequent visits made by Special Agent
McCarthy to Las Vegas, endeavoring to secure information from
Bennett that would lead to the arrest and conviction of the
DeAutremont brothers, in connection with the holdup of Southern
Pacific Train # 13, at Siskiyou, Ore., on October 11th, 1923.

On January 7th, I went to Las Vegas as prearranged with Mr. E.
F. Dupray, Attorney, representing Bennett, where I conferred
with the latter, in presence of Mr. Dupray at his office.

I find that Bennett is employed by the Union Pacific System
working on a section at a place called Moapa, and on his own voli-
tion he stated that regardless of any assistance from anyone, he intended to go to Siskiyou in the vicinity of the holdup, about the
15th of this month. I then questioned Bennett as to how he learned
that the DeAutremont brothers were the parties that committed
this depredation, and he stated that while beating his way on a
freight train on the Union Pacific, that he met a party who was doing the same thing, and during their conversation this party mentioned to him that prior to this holdup the DeAutremont brothers
used his car for carrying loot to a hiding place about 100 miles
from the scene of the holdup of train # 13, and that he was
positive that they are hiding in this same rendezvous again.

At this time Mr. Dupary (sic) intercepted our conversation by
stating that before Bennett would disclose the town or location
that they should have some written authority that would protect
him and Bennett in case that this investigation lead to the apprehension and conviction of the parties mentioned. In view of
this, Bennett did not disclose the name of the town, but did state
that it was located on the main line of the Southern Pacific and
that the DeAutremont brothers were hiding about 60 miles from
this town and that they come into the latter to get supplies when
necessary. He further stated that he was never in that part of the
country, but from his conversation with the party who claims to
have known where these DeAutremonts are, he drew a map, which
he would not have any difficulty with, in going to the place.

The Post Office authorities were advised of this exciting development in the case and in addition to the above report sent by Post
Office Inspector F. E. Smith he had Mr. Bennett sign an affidavit
regarding his statements:

State of Nevada
County of Clark

Lewis G. Bennett, being first duly sworn deposes and says: That
I was out of funds and was beating my way on a freight train from
Moapa to Las Vegas, Nev., that I met a man who claimed to be a
particular friend of the DeAutremont Brothers; that this was
about December 1st, 1923; that this man mentioned the fact that
there was a big reward out for these brothers who assisted this
man by paying off a mortgage which he owed on his machine, and
he in return took the DeAutremont Brothers out to their hiding
place; that this man imparted to me the name of the town to
which these men went after their provisions, and that they had
their location out about 60 miles from said town in the mountains;
that I know the direction that this hiding place lays from the
town, and he said that it was due East and that the town is located
on the Southern Pacific Railway in the State of Oregon; that this
man claimed that there were four men on the job and that an older
man furnished the brains for the jobs that were pulled; that this
man claimed the hiding place to be in a cave, and if my offer to
assist is not accepted by the Southern Pacific Co., it is my inten-
tion to go to Oregon and endeavor to locate the men myself; that
in my present financial condition I will be unable to go to Oregon
for about one month.

Subscribed and sworn to
before me at Byron, Nevada
this 11th day of January 1924   Lewis G. Bennett
                                                    AFFIANT

F. E. Smith
POST OFFICE INSPECTOR.

Several weeks later, following numerous other discussions and
transportation to Oregon, it was decided that Bennett was merely
blessed with considerable imagination, indicated by Mr.
O'Connell's sardonic communication:

San Francisco, Calif. Mar. 19, 1924
Mr. Louis G. Bennett
% D. H. Looney
Jefferson, Ore.

Dear Sir:

Yours, March 16th. I regret that your clue ran out on you, but it
seems that you are ambitious, and it is apparent that you like to
travel.
Being that you are going to South America, should you locate
the bandits there, I wish you would cable me.

Yours truly

D. O'Connell

Frequently, communications came from individuals offering their outstanding services (for a fee generally) as special agents in locating the missing suspects:

Nov. 3, 1923
Salem, Ore.

Mr. Dan O'Connell
Southern Pacific Agent
Ashland, Ore.

Dear Sir:

A few days after the Southern Pacific tragedy, I was talking to Mr. LaVoy of Portland. He was in my office twice, and also with Mr. Baker of Salem. I told them I was well acquainted with the DeAutremont family and if I could find the boys I am almost positive they would place themselves in my hands for safe keeping until they could have a hearing, guilty or not guilty. Would recognize them at a distance or any place. Also told them if the Company would put up my expense, against my time, I would go out and make an effort to land them, and in case I found them if guilty would divide the reward 50-50, same as expense and time spent. I have been in the criminal and insane work for about 26 years. Lived in Salem for 28 years.
Enclosed you will find a letter from Mr. DeAutremont.

Sincerely yours

H. A. Rawson
462 State St.
Salem, Oreg.

The following letter was enclosed:

Eugene, Oregon Oct. 25, 1923

Dear Friend:

Your letter of sympathy and cheer touches a cord in the heart of a man that words cannot convey. To bear a cross of this kind and in this way is hard, and Oh so cruel, but God still lives, His will be done, but it is Oh so cruel. My boys may be dead on some lonely mountain side, time will tell. But this I know they never did that terrible deed. I trust you fully, Oh, if only knew my boys are to aid and council them and be with them but this is maddening, this suspense, I only pray my God for strength to bear my load. If you hear of the boys, go to them, Percy Varney will also. May God bless you and yours.

Good by

Paul DeAutremont

Wife and children well, and baby a big boy now.

Sheriff of Jackson County, Oregon
Jacksonville, Oregon

February 25th, 1924

Mr. D. O'Connell
Chief Special Agent, S.P. RR Co.,
San Francisco, Calif.

Dear Sir:

I am enclosing herewith a letter received from Eureka, California from one Wm. E. Rodney.

I am forwarding the original to you and will retain the copy for my file. Although this sounds a little fishy it may be well to get in touch with the Sheriff at Eureka regarding the case.

This letter came to us under a special delivery stamp.

Yours very truly

C. E. Terrill, Sheriff,
by L. D. Forncrook
Deputy

(letter enclosed)

Eureka, Calif., Feb. 20, 1924

Sheriff - Medford, Oregon.

Dear Sir:

This letter is from one who you do not know or seen. I am a hobo. I have, at one time, had a good many friends and a chance to be someone, but throwed my chances away like the fool that I am, and I have for a long time tried to find a way to get back on the right road, and now my chance has come, but I need your help.

Where you come in on this matter is this - if you care to get the Train Robbers of #13, wire me fifty dollars to the Humboldt Savings Bank here at Eureka, so I can come to Medford. The sooner I get there the better it will be, and if you will do as I want, why we will have the boys before this time next month. If you will do as I want and will trust me, why I will lay a bet, I will bring in the boys by the tenth of next month. If I am a hobo, I am honest. For this part I say ask Sheriff Ross here in Eureka and Abe Ruer, Judge Cabinass in San Francisco, California.

This letter may look funny to you but if you will send the fifty dollars and will do as I say, I will bring home the "Baken". All hobos are not fools or dishonest, so take a chance. Will go 50-50 on the reward. Answer at once, hoping you will send the $50.00 and take me up on the matter at once. I await your answer

Yours truly
William E. Rodney
Eureka Humboldt Co., Cal.

Please excuse poor spelling.

A flood of crank letters poured in, some with rather wild theories of what had happened and why. Other speculations also had to be checked out, even though they seemed a waste of time:

Mr. C. B. Welter,
P.O. Inspector,
Portland.

Dear Sir:

Yours of 18th Feb. at hand and contents carefully noted. Yes sir, I did make statement regarding the DeAutremont boys and the train 13 blow up on Oct. 11, 1923, at tunnel 13, and you called as a hold up it is and never was hold up. Called blew up hereafter you know that I.W.W's are at war with us American Legion, and it was to blow up the members of the American Legion on their way to convention at San Francisco.

I came to your office to give you all the information on December 14th, 1923, but the young man was there at the time snubbed me by not giving me chance to explain. He told me plainly that my help was not needed so I get a little discouraged and as I had to see Dr. Lindville I went to see him, gave him dope for his work, which I am sure he found correct.

I don't go after these men for the reward alone, it is war between American Legion and I.W.W's. One of the American Legionairies (sic) and I am living on government homestead 10 miles from Port Orford so I got the first news of the blow up on the 17th of October, 1923. As I was in the post office did not look right to me at minute I learned that it was No. 13 that they blew up as from long service with S. P. Co. I know that 13 never has any money as 11 and 53 are only trains with money, so on the 18th I goes to Crescent City on 19th to Orick. In Orick I learned from an Indian that on early morning of the 12th the 3 cars came together from Yreka and two cars red and black after taking oil at once started toward Crescent City, one car went toward Trinidad, 3 men and 1 young woman in it, 2 cars going to Crescent City, red had 4 men in it; black had 3 in it. What Indian said I felt sure I had struck right trace, but I went to Medford, got in contact with members of I.W.W. learned from them that 17 people were in plot to blow up American Legion train in this way to convention at San Francisco. 5 autos took part in blow up. 1 went to Medford, 1 toward McCloud, 3 toward Yreka, 2 women were in this undertaking; one's name is Tuella from Sacramento, others names I have not learned at yet. But I will if I live. I went back to Orick and Oct. 22nd, started North, found trail of two cars, clear to Marshfield; red car was left then black one. I nosed as far as Reedsport, then lost it there.

On Oct. 27th I went back to Port Orford to get ready to take up the trail; as soon as I could, on Nov. 2, I started again. Went and consulted people at Eugene, discovered that DeAutremont brothers had during month of August and September been seen going from Eugene toward coast with two pack horses heavily loaded, same time twice a week and once at least, then on Nov. 6th I got to working among I.W.W's at Marshfield, North Bend, Neal, Lakeside, Reedsport and Powers, learned from I.W.W. members why the train was to be blown up, at Nov. 11, 1919, in Centralia, Wash. that is and then where it started when 4 American Legion members were killed. DeAutremonts are to be kept in coast by I.W.W. till spring as they are going to start lot of trouble in May all along the coast. I was on my way to San Francisco on Jan. 5th to see Mr. Dyer of S. P. and also U.S.S.S. man when I met auto accident on way in which I got pretty much bruised. I dont know when I will be able to take trail again as I have used up all my spare money and am not able to follow them for time being.

Yes sir, as late as Dec. 28th, 1923, DeAutremont boys were still in their hiding place about 60 miles toward coast from Eugene. Old man DeAutremont looks very simple, but take it from me he is as shrewd as holy father can make them. I.W.W. members are in daily communication with the old man De and boys. Did you look up Murphys the Florence Banks robbers record where was he on Oct. 11th, and who was the black robber that got away. Until I know who you are I will not tell you more than this, because members of I W W get their confidence be very enthusiastic at it and you learn all about the DeAutremont boys and spring work for them. Go to Dr. Lindville, have him to O.K. you in your return letter to me and if I find that you are true blue I then give you some more information on this same matter as to why is that failure is in capturing those criminals. As soon as I am well I am going to ask my friends to lend me some money and I will get them fellows, just the same, and say now remember that I am first class I W W members till our trouble this year is over and revenge is complete.

Watch old man De closely and put some good man in job, one who is able to read between lines and you will sooner or later get right lead. We are going to have lot of trouble with wobbs this year so watch out. This is only briefly stated, far from being complete. I am yours

Very sincerely,

John E. Slovey,
Port Orford, Ore.

PS When I said your men or you have to be an I W W in order to reach these fellows, yourself among them as one and have same enthusiasm for this cause, you see I am not I W W and never could be one, yet I am in all their secrets and carry pass book. If you are interested and I hear from you I shall give you little more dope as we go along. If I had enough money I would be on road again in first part of March or as soon as my arm would be in shape to travel, to get all of these fellows. We must go patiently and with care but we will get them and I hope it would cause any more loss of lives.

I am sincerely yours,

John E. Slovey

Unquestionably, little further time was spent checking Mr. Slovey's conjectures.

Some individuals dreamed up elaborate schemes to achieve publicity for their business, such as the incident of a letter reportedly found by P.P. Fisher, in Salem, addressed to Monsieur Jean DeAutremont, 11 Rue Palace, Paris, France. As it turned out, Mr. Fisher was manager of the Red Top Cab Co., in Salem, and merely anxious to achieve some publicity for the company.

In June 1926, the Postmaster at Lima, Ohio, advised that the watch described as belonging to Roy DeAutremont had been repaired during Nov. 1925, by W. M. Northrup, a jeweler at Lima. Several agents descended on Lima and found Mr. Northrup well thought of and considered to be a reliable person. However, upon thorough investigation, it was ascertained the entire story was pure fabrication. Actually, as it was learned much later, upon discovering the watch so specifically described in the wanted posters, Roy had thrown it into a river.

There never was a grander time for amateur detectives and thousands of letters flooded the authorities with requests for pictures, information, etc.

Hillside, Ky. Feb. 7, 1925
Chief Special Agent, S. P. Co.
San Francisco, Calif.

Dear Sirs:

I have been and am at present doing detective work for the Illinois Central R. R. Co. I would like to have photos of the ones who robbed a train on your road and spoke of taking a long sea voyage. I think one of trio of your men are here. The mines in this and adjoining countries are working open shop and they have been Union so there are lots of Comers and Goers around here.

Did any parties by name of Irvin Nash or James O. Lear ever give you any trouble. I would like to have photos of the mail robbers by return mail.

Yours resp.
Estle L. Hastings

Tim T. Keliher, Chief special agent, I.C.R.R., advised that Mr. Hastings had merely applied at Illinois Central for a job and he was "the product of some detective school and his information can be taken accordingly". Graduates from other types of mail order educational institutions also endeavored to put their training to practical use.

North Kansas City, Mo.
Sept. 23, 1924

C. E. Terrill
Sheriff
Jackson County
Jacksonville, Oregon

Dear Sir:

Could you please send me more information about:
    Roy DeAutremont
    Finger print classification
    31 I M M 14
    28 O I I 17

I am a Finger Print Expert trained by the U.S. School of Finger Prints and am ready to take up any case that is open. The information that I would like to have is his home address and the address of a "buddy" of his; the name of any Secret Sociaty (sic) and any other information that you think would be helpful.

I would also like to have a warrent for his arrest.

> Very sincerely yours
>
> Mr. Lloyd M. Williams
> 1031 23rd Street
> North Kansas City, Mo.

> West Frankfort, Ill.
> Jan. 11th, 1924

C.E. Terrill, Sheriff:

Dear Sir:

I am writting in regards of three "Wanted Violaters." Name follows:

Roy DeAutremont
Ray DeAutremont
Hugh DeAutremont
    Case No. 57885-D

I am connected with the Secret Service and I have been informed that these three fellows were seen in Biggers Arkansas, looking for employment, but only stayed one night in Biggers. It being a month ago since they were seen in Biggers.

I would like to receive photo and full descriptions of these wanted violaters and full details of same.

> Yours truly,
> O. J. King, F. P. E.
> 808 East Clark St.,
> West Frankfort, Ill.

Correspondence school detectives and over-imaginative individuals may have run the authorities ragged, checking out an avalanche of reports. But, for pure imagination and flair of execution, a prison inmate, one C. R. Williams, topped them all.

In February 1924, while in jail at The Dalles, Oregon, charged with robbing the Mosier Valley Bank on Nov. 27, 1923, of $917.50, he claimed to possess valuable information about the unsolved DeAutremont case. While he seemed reluctant to discuss it in great detail at that time, later, after being sent to the Oregon State Penitentiary, he frequently hinted at this knowledge of the crime. Warden J. W. Lillie, learning of these comments, became extremely interested in the story and advised Governor Walter Pierce of the matter. A meeting was arranged, and they were greatly impressed with his obvious sincerity and apparent acquaintanceship with the three fugitives.

Officials questioned Ted Madronas (Ted the Greek), one of the two men who were involved with Williams in the bank robbery. Madronas claimed Williams had slain the three DeAutremonts, along with Roy (Alabam) Vincent, the third bank robber.

Agent Maurice L. Coturri verified that Williams was working during Oct. 1923 for Whitney Lumber Co. in Garibaldi, and therefore could not have participated in the crime; in fact, Coturri was extremely suspicious of the entire story but was overruled by his superiors.

According to Williams' story, shortly after the holdup, he had met the twins near Shaniko, at the ranch of Bill Gott, a criminal friend; he stole a Cadillac car and drove them to Pocatello, Idaho, and further stated that through his relationship with Gott, the DeAutremonts could undoubtedly be located. In return for release from prison, he offered to assist in finding the missing brothers.

Williams was provided with money and given a temporary release from the penitentiary, to visit Gott. He returned in a few days, declaring that the fugitives were hid out at the O-Bar Ranch in a remote location near Denver, Colorado, but that through the friend's assistance, he could arrange to meet them, ostensibly with the objective of persuading them to return to Oregon and help in robbing the O.W.R. & N. train #18 on the Deschutes River.

Despite the suspicions of Coturri, the story was so convincing that in April 1926 Governor Pierce issued a conditional pardon; the warden advanced more money, and the Southern Pacific furnished Williams a round trip ticket to Denver. Post Office inspectors were assigned to follow him and apprehend the suspects as they came west. While in Denver, Williams requested more money and Inspector Jefferson gave him an additional $40. Williams immediately disappeared, leaving behind a rumpled room as though a struggle had taken place. The return portion of the ticket was found lying in the street in front of the hotel.

A substantial number of very red faces were left behind from the efforts of this highly proficient liar and con man. Later, Williams made the very foolish mistake of returning to Oregon and was recognized. He was arrested in Portland, the conditional pardon was revoked and he was sent back to Salem to serve the balance of his sentence. It can be readily assumed that he received no further favors from Warden Lillie.

Williams claimed the reason he didn't keep his bargain was that the Post Office inspectors stayed too close and he was afraid the DeAutremonts would find him out and kill him. The officials pointed out to him that when he had given them the slip in Denver he had endeavored to leave the impression of foul play and perhaps even of his death.

An inspector was sent to England in an effort to have circulars distributed there, as well as to Australia, New Zealand and other

British possessions, although this was not totally successful. Inspector Jefferson then made a personal trip to Australia to obtain the cooperation of the authorities there. Inspector C. W. B. Long of the Austin Division (Texas) specialized on the search throughout Central and South America, visiting various countries and keeping in contact with people there, in an effort to track down every possible lead. Even reports from the Orient had to be carefully checked out.

The Canadian authorities were extremely cooperative during the long and extensive search. Both English and French reward posters were furnished and Canadian postal officials distributed them throughout the country. Apparent clues and tips came from the remotest corners of Canada, and the Royal Canadian Mounted Police frequently journeyed to those areas investigating the reports. The U.S. authorities were highly complimentary regarding the splendid assistance received from the Canadian officials.

It was well-established that the brothers were avid readers and regularly frequented libraries, so extensive coverage of these was effected. Personal visits were made by officers to all libraries in the 105 largest cities of the U.S. and a circular was placed in the hands of each employee at these libraries. A special effort was also made with the law enforcement organizations in these same cities, each officer personally receiving a wanted poster picturing and describing the trio.

All Army, Navy, Marine Corps and Coast Guard recruiting offices were alerted and provided with reward posters for appropriate display.

The captains of all ships of consequence in both Pacific and Atlantic ports received circulars, together with a letter requesting their crews be interviewed, to see if anyone remembered the fugitives, or if they had been seen in any foreign port of call. The same letter and circulars were also sent to all ship captains on the Great Lakes.

Reports on the fugitives almost overwhelmed those in charge of the search; frequently many tips were received on the same day. Each had to be carefully checked out but none proved valid.

There was a standing joke at the Postal Department that, whenever an inspector wanted a field trip or a few days vacation, he merely dug into the pile of reports on the case, seeking one near his objective and then went investigating the DeAutremont case.

There were those, too, who wanted a free trip to Oregon or craved the glamour of personal notoriety and assumed a confession was the easy solution. Each of these had to be carefully investigated.

Despite the staggering number of clues the brothers had bumblingly scattered throughout the State of Oregon prior to the crime not one single tangible trace of their whereabouts had cropped up. Seemingly, like three phantoms in the night, they had vanished. Many people were convinced that they were dead. Weeks

During the Sesqui-Centennial Exposition at Philadelphia in 1926, dramatic pictures of the bloody crime were displayed in hope that they might trigger recognition of the wanted men.

turned into months and months into years. Descriptive circulars blanketed the world.

On May 6, 1924, a partially decomposed body of a young man was discovered in the Rogue River. Inasmuch as it somewhat resembled the DeAutremonts, Paul DeAutremont was brought to Medford to view the body. He stunned everyone by identifying it as the remains of his son Hugh. A short time later, when provided with further information regarding the body, he agreed it was not his missing son.

An excited report was received from Rockland, Maine, advising a Roy DeAutremont had worked in a barber shop there for about a week and Ray and Hugh were staying with him, all using their real names. While it appeared obviously absurd, it, like thousands of other tips, was carefully checked out and found false.

1924 passed, 1925 came and went, then 1926, and still not one factual lead to their location had turned up. More and more people were certain the boys were not alive, perhaps had committed suicide in one last defiant act against society as a result of their unsuccessful venture into crime and its bloody aftermath.

During 1926, a booth was maintained at the Sesqui-Centennial Exposition at Philadelphia, where pictures of the wanted men were displayed, together with dramatic scenes of the crime. 85,000 reward posters were distributed to people attending the Exposition.

Newspapers and free-lance writers were urged to do feature articles on the unsolved crime, including pictures of the vanished threesome and a description of their personal characteristics. News bulletins were regularly issue by the Chief Postal Inspector and the Postmaster General, doing everything possible to keep pictures of the wanted men before the public. Even radio stations were used, being requested to broadcast detailed descriptions of the fugitive brothers, quite an innovation for the time.

As Roy had at one time been an attendant in an insane asylum, all such institutions employing male attendants were circularized. Jails and penal institutions in the U.S. and throughout the world were provided posters, in the event the men might be found imprisoned on other charges.

Circulars were placed in almost every rooming or apartment house and hotel in the larger cities. All dentists and opticians received a copy describing the dental work and glasses of the twins. Lumber camps, employment agencies and police officers were sent new posters at regular intervals.

The years passed. Reward poster after reward poster was printed. As additional scraps of information about the fugitives were received, they were incorporated into the new posters. Circulars were printed in Spanish, French, German, Dutch and Portugese, but no clue to the whereabouts of the wanted men proved worthwhile.

Huge numbers of circulars were printed and distributed:

1st circular — printed and distributed on October 11, 1923, within a few hours of the hold up. No identity for the suspects. 2,000 copies . . . cost $75.00.

2nd circular — printed October 13, 1923. Still no identity on the suspects. 10,000 copies . . . cost $100.00.

3rd circular — printed October 21, 1923. Photos of the twins were pasted on the posters by hand. While Hugh was listed as a suspect, his picture was not included. Bernard LeChance was also listed as a suspect on this poster, although he was soon absolved of any complicity in the crime. 5,000 copies . . . cost $600.00.

4th circular — printed October 24, 1923. 30,500 copies . . . cost $220.00.

5th circular — printed November 13, 1923. 40,000 copies . . . cost $38.00.

6th circular — printed November 13, 1923. 10,000 copies . . . cost $18.00. (Spanish)

7th circular — printed November 30, 1923. 4,000 copies . . . cost $8.00 (Spanish)

8th circular — printed June 2, 1924. 100,000 copies . . . cost $243.58.

9th circular — printed April 10, 1926. 2,500 copies . . . cost $50.00. This contained fingerprint information and copies were sent to all fingerprint identification bureaus in the world.

10th circular — printed April 21, 1926. 24,000 copies . . . cost $35.00. Sent to masters of ships on Atlantic and Pacific Coasts.

11th circular — printed May 17, 1926. 1,000,000 copies . . . cost (unknown). This was the poster seen by Sgt. Reynolds and which resulted in the capture of Hugh.

12th circular — printed July 23, 1926. 140,000 copies . . . cost $361.37.

13th circular — printed July 23, 1926. 260,000 copies . . . cost $670.80.

14th circular — printed December 1926. 20,000 copies . . . cost $207.31 (French)

15th circular — printed December 1926. 80,000 copies . . . cost $417.99 (Spanish)
16th circular — printed Jan 27, 1927. 100,000 copies . . . cost $298.00.

17th circular — printed February 1927. This was a leaflet sent with the Postal Guide supplements for display in Post Offices and postal stations.

18th circular - printed April 1927. 10,000 copies . . . cost $128.21 (Dutch)

19th circular - printed April 1927. 10,000 copies . . . cost $128.78 (German)

20th circular - printed April 11, 1927. 500,000 copies . . . cost $2,-129.55.

21st circular - printed April 1927. 20,000 copies . . . cost $207.84 (French)

22nd circular - printed April 1927. 100,000 copies . . . cost $595.86 (Spanish)

23rd circular - printed April 1927. 50,000 copies . . . cost $300.00. (Portuguese)

Reports continued to pour in from all corners of the world. A barber in Puerto Rico reported that Roy had been in his shop but never returned. During March, 1925, F. E. Whitney, Acting Inspector in charge of the Spokane Division Post Office, wrote to O'Connell, advising that Inspector Welter, of the Spokane Division, and Inspector Madiera, of the S.F. Division (who spoke fluent Spanish) had visited Nicaragua and had made an investigation at Blue Fields and other areas, including Colon, Panama and Honduras. No trace of the wanted men was found.

Reports were repeatedly received that one or more of the fugitives was employed in Louisiana and Arkansas, but on checking each proved erroneous.

Traveling magazine salesmen were constantly harrassed, particularly in small communities, being frequently arrested and tossed into jail until their identities could be established. Numerous

Thomas Reynolds recognized the reward poster picture as being that of a soldier he had served with in the Philippine Islands.

"New Idea Magazine" salesmen decided they didn't really care much for that work, under the circumstances.

During March, 1926, Governor Pierce of Oregon, later to smart with very personal embarrassment from the C. R. Williams incident, arranged to have still an additional $500 reward offered on the wanted men. The total official reward, at that point, was $15,900.

On June 12, 1926, newspaper headlines announced that the twins had been captured in Juneau, Alaska, and were in jail there. Reportedly, Hugh had escaped the arresting officers, but it was expected that he too would be in custody soon. The arrested men gave the aliases of A. Erickson, of Detroit, and J. Martin, of Los Angeles, according to the arresting officers. As it turned out, they were still not the elusive DeAutrements.

Many ex-convicts and criminals were suspected of having been involved in some fashion, with the crime, and frequently law enforcement agencies made some rather specific allegations in their wanted notices. When Henry C. (Scarface) Young was charged with assaulting and robbing Sprague Riegel, of Medford, it was also prominently mentioned that he was suspected of being involved with the DeAutremonts. Apparently, Mr. Young believed that the best defense in this instance was a good offense. In any event, he filed suit against the S.P. for $50,000 and against the Medford *News* for $10,000, stating their false accusations had cost him his wife and homestead, although not necessarily in that order. The ploy did not work.

The authorities were not alone in the receipt of anonymous crank letters, as various members of the DeAutremont family regularly received vicious, nasty letters. Some related gory details of the boys' deaths, others berated them for being related to such unholy monsters or accused them of being in league with the Pope in some terrible scheme against Protestants, etc.

The search continued.

On July 2, 1926, William H. Stone, the Southern Pacific agent in San Francisco, was in his office when a Sergeant Thomas Reynolds insisted upon seeing him personally. To his astonishment, the soldier advised him that Hugh DeAutremont was using the name of James C. Price and, at that moment, serving as a Private in Company B, 31st Infantry, in Manila, P.I. After listening to the Sergeant's story and asking numerous questions, Stone excitedly took him to the nearby Postal Inspector's office, where the story was repeated. It seemed too good to be true.

While a host of false clues and tips had been checked out over the years, at long last this one did have the appearance of being worthwhile and an immediate investigation was launched.

Private Price's enlistment papers were examined and, although they provided no additional information or substantiation of the sergeant's statements, several items did appear to warrant further investigation. For example, Houston, Texas, was given as his birthplace but no record of his birth could be found. William Adams, the person to be notified in case of an emergency, could not be located or identified.

These doubtful items, by themselves, were far from conclusive, but a recommendation was made on November 17, 1926, that Inspector Fred Smith of the San Francisco division be sent to Manila, P.I., to determine definitely if Private James C. Price was, in fact, the long elusive Hugh DeAutremont.

On February 11, 1927, day rooms at the 31st Infantry Regiment buzzed with the information that the personable Private James C. Price, from Company B, was in actuality the notorious Hugh DeAutremont, wanted in the States for the brutal murder of four men during an attempted train robbery. Incredulous friends of the young soldier were stunned as he departed for San Francisco in custody.

Oddly enough, within a few days after Hugh's arrest, another soldier at Angel Island reported that a soldier in Co. C, 31st Infantry, P.I., greatly resembled Hugh. He was advised that Hugh was already in custody.

Arriving in San Francisco on March 17, 1927, Hugh was formally arrested and confined in the U.S. Disciplinary Barracks on Alcatraz Island for interrogation. Hugh's long flight had ended, half way around the world from where it began. However, the twins were still at large, with no clue as to their whereabouts, for while Hugh admitted his identity, he steadfastly claimed to have no information whatsoever regarding the whereabouts of his two brothers.

Sergeant Reynolds and Hugh were brought together in San Francisco for one last brief encounter but the confrontation produced little excitement, other than a laconical greeting between the two.

"Hello, Price."

"Hello, Sergeant."

Nor did Reynolds offer to return the watch and overcoat which he was supposed to have borrowed from Private James C. Price, in Manila. Perhaps the feeling of having betrayed a comrade was why Reynolds reportedly squandered the reward money he eventually received in a rather quick, riotous fashion and reenlisted in the Army.

Chapter 5

DeAutremont Family Background

There still are no sure methods of recognizing the criminally inclined, and there certainly was no early indication that any of the DeAutremont boys were apt to be involved in serious criminal activity. They were raised as Catholics and attended church quite regularly. Even though there was considerable dissention between their mother and a somewhat improvident father, it was no worse than most other homes of the same period and much better than many.

Paul DeAutremont, the father, was a high-strung, moody man, of French ancestry, while the mother, Belle, was a more stolid, steady, optimistic individual, of German background and deeply religious.

At the time the twins were born, March 31, 1900, there was already one son, and the home was near Williamsburg, Iowa, where the father was working as a barber. Barbering at Williamsburg was not overly profitable and, shortly after the twins' birth, the family moved to Mena, Arkansas, where, during 1904, the fourth son, Hugh, was born. The father continued working as a barber.

When Hugh was around 6 months old, the family again moved, to Colorado, settling initially near Cripple Creek, later moving to various other mining camps in the state. The father kept on barbering, although he also periodically did odd jobs of wall papering and painting. While in Colorado, Lee, the last of the five boys, was born.

Sometime during 1909, the elder DeAutremont read some promotional material about a land development at Lakewood, New Mexico, some 60 miles from Roswell. His enthusiastic interest in the proposition was aroused and as a result he sold out in Colorado and purchased a plot of land "sight unseen" from a Mr. Fairchild. Packing his wife and five sons, together with his worldly possessions, into a covered wagon, he made the lengthy drive across the desert to the site of his new land home-site. Following an arduous trip, with the older boys walking most of the way, they arrived at Roswell shortly before Christmas 1909.

Paul DeAutremont, as well as his sons were all very fleet of foot. The boys were always proud of the fact that, soon after arriving, during the community Christmas celebration, their father won the

big foot race held there. The local people jokingly referred to him as
"The Colorado Race Horse."

In short order, DeAutremont discovered the land promotion was
mostly a "blue sky" scheme and that he had been thoroughly
hornswoggled by the promoter. However, there they were, and it
was necessary to make the best of the situation. He rented a farm
(the Gosset farm) some 7 miles west of Lakewood.

Again in a strange chain of circumstances and ifs—that particular year was extremely dry. Their farm of green, growing things
was surrounded by barren, dry cattle country. Their small artesian
well was the envy of the area and bad blood quickly developed
between the cattle ranchers and the "foreign newcomers." In addition to the hungry, thirsty cattle tearing down their fences, the cow-
punchers would lift the barbed wire, staple it to the top of the posts
and let the cattle into the fields, soon destroying much of the crops.

While no one was shot, DeAutremont did pack a rifle part of the
time and there was great concern in the family about the possibility
of the ranchers hiring someone to shoot him on a dark night.

Ironically, what crops were finally harvested were consigned to a
commission man, who wound up with more commissions than sales.
Perhaps it was at this point that blighting resentments at social injustice began creeping into young Ray's mind . . . the mis-
represented land scheme . . . the commission agent . . . the
ranchers' cattle . . . resentments which in later years were to create
a burning concern for the working man's lot and add dangerous
sparks to his discontent.

In any event, the frustration and failure of this venture created
great family tensions, with continuing and bitter arguments
between the parents. The farm was eventually abandoned and the
family moved to Lakewood, where a small inheritance of Mrs.
DeAutremont's was used to purchase a store. Unfortunately, a
rapidly declining economy in the area didn't make that much of a
success either. Wrangling between the parents grew worse and,
after one particularly unpleasant episode in which Mrs. DeAutremont was knocked down, she had her husband arrested. This embittered him, and after his release from jail he left the family and
returned to Victor, Colorado.

Mrs. DeAutremont subsequently leased out the store and rejoin-
ed her husband in Colorado. However, the controversies continued,
and a couple of years later she and the boys returned to New Mexico.

DeAutremont did, apparently, make one more effort to save the
marriage, for he returned to New Mexico shortly thereafter and
bought another farm, on credit, near Lake McMillan. It was while
the family was living on this farm that the twins left home. They

were only about 16 or 17 years old at the time, but the continuous squabbling between their parents made them decide to go out on their own.

Mr. DeAutremont's new farm was no more successful than his previous farming venture, and before long he gave up the place and again left the family. Eventually, he settled in Oregon, where he later remarried and worked as a barber for many years.

Ray left first, going to Oklahoma, where he was soon followed by Roy. They both attended barber school and worked as waiters in a nearby boarding house. Both regularly went to Sunday Mass. Barbering didn't particularly appeal to Ray and after a couple of months he gave it up and returned home. His restlessness continued though, and he soon left again, traveling up into the Middlewest and then on to the Northwest, picking up whatever odd jobs he could find.

It must have been a difficult period for the untrained, small of stature, 17-year-old youngster. In riding freight trains from one town to another in search of jobs, he spent a great deal of time around "hobo jungles" near the railroad tracks, becoming thoroughly exposed to the agitators and organizers of the radically oriented I.W.W., so high in favor with migratory workers of the period. There were great abuses of power by many of the big employers and the "Industrial Workers of the World" seemingly offered answers to the more downtrodden class of men, eagerly searching for solutions to their problems. The idealistic theories advanced by some of the articulate members of the I.W.W. apparently had great appeal to the inexperienced youngster, who was having trouble obtaining a regular, worthwhile job and saw thousands of others in a similar plight. By 1918, when Ray arrived in Portland, he was a proud carrier of the red membership card of the "Wobblies" and, even after going to work in a Vancouver (Wash.) shipyard in 1919, he was a vocal supporter of the cause.

Working conditions in many logging camps in the northwest, at that time, left a lot to be desired, and some camps made the title "timber beast" seem rather appropriate when applied to the occupants. The food, living conditions, and employment policies were in most instances deplorable.

The organization was not universally liked by workers, many of whom were philosophically opposed to striking, and who derisively referred to members of the I.W.W. as "Wobblies" or the "I Won't Work" bunch. Nevertheless, it is generally credited with materially helping to improve the lot of the loggers, dockworkers and cannery employees, and its rapid growth began to create concern among many of the big timber and shipping interests. Some of these employers were rather crusty characters themselves, which resulted in a number of very strong, and, frequently, downright illegal, efforts to put the I.W.W. out of operation.

The blatant Bolshevik leanings of some I.W.W. leaders also gave it much bad publicity, frightening off a considerable portion of its early supporters. *(Author's note: I have been personally acquainted with men who were working in Washington during the period and many of them secretly carried cards from both the I.W.W. and the (employer sponsored) Loyal Legion of Loggers and Lumbermen, or the Four Ls, as it was called. By carefully predetermining which organization was on top in a given camp, they had a better chance of getting a job.)*

On November 11, 1919, the newly-formed American Legion Post in Centralia, Washington, held its first Armistice Day Parade. While the motives of that particular parade have been in deep controversy ever since, the facts are that the Legionnaires' parade path did pass in front of the I.W.W. headquarters and, for whatever reason, it did stop in front of the headquarters. It is not specifically known which faction started the trouble but a flurry of shots broke out and three legionnaires fell dead. A few minutes later a number of irate veterans cornered an I.W.W. member, Wesley Everest (a veteran himself), who shot his nearest pursuer before surrendering. That night there was a mysterious failure of city power and during the darkness a mob dragged Everest from jail. The following day his bullet punctured body was found dangling from a nearby bridge.

As a result of the tragic confrontation, eight members of the I.W.W. were sent to prison and a regular "witch hunt" took place in the state. More than 1,000 men and women were rounded up and thrown into jail on a multitude of flimsy charges. Many were charged with "Criminal Syndicalism" which often consisted of nothing more sinister than having a red I.W.W. membership card in their possession.

As a result of this statewide sweep, on November 17, 1919, Ray DeAutremont was arrested in a cheap Vancouver, Washington, hotel and tossed into the Clark County jail.

There is considerable controversy at this point, the officials claiming he was active as a minor officer in the organization and Ray contending that he merely was a member.

In any event, it appears considerable pressure was applied to the 19-year-old to testify against others and on refusing, he was subjected to a great deal of abuse to force him to change his mind. After several days in jail, and what he considered inhuman treatment, including frequent periods of solitary confinement, together with a diet of bread and water, he persuaded another inmate to join him and tried to escape from custody. Quickly recaptured, he was then charged with breaking jail, in addition to the earlier charges. *(There is a strong possibility he was permitted to escape with a planned capture.)*

Roy left home shortly after Ray, but most of his time had been spent in or near Oklahoma. He had attended barber college in

Oklahoma City and, upon finishing, went to work as a barber in nearby Texola, Oklahoma. Later, a friend persuaded him to move to Lawton, Oklahoma, and work in a shop there. This was during World War I and nearby Ft. Sill was a booming Army camp. Before long Roy opened a shop at the 78th Field Artillery and operated as the post barber until the outfit left for France.

Roy later stated that he had tried to enlist in the Student Army Training Corps, but was turned down due to his lack of education. While this may be questionable, he did move to Weatherford, Oklahoma, and enrolled in the Normal School for a term, working evenings and Saturdays as a barber to earn his way. (Roy's total higher education consisted of this period at the Normal School, a short time at the Lawton High School and later, a part of a year at the Salem High School, Salem, Oregon.)

Although only 19 at the time, Roy's eyes began to trouble him, forcing him to quit barbering. He returned to his mother's place in New Mexico, but, unable to find steady work, soon returned to Ft. Sill, where he again opened a barber shop on the base.

He was still operating the shop at Ft. Sill when a frantic letter was received from his father in Salem, Oregon, advising him of Ray's arrest and pleading with him to come and help.

There was an extremely close fraternal bond between the twins, and without delay, Roy immediately closed his shop, liquidated everything possible, and with around $100, caught the train to Oregon.

On arriving in Salem, he was joined by his father and they went on to Vancouver, where Ray was in jail. An interview was arranged with Judge Holden, who had sat on the case. Desperately, they pleaded with him to release Ray into Roy's custody. The Judge was adamant, and, despite their impassioned pleas, on May 12, 1920, the 20-year old Ray was sentenced to the Washington State Reformatory at Monroe to serve one year for criminal syndicalism.

One of the major planks in the I.W.W. philosophy was that "the working man did not receive justice," and this became a burning conviction with the resentful young man who felt he had committed no crime whatsoever. He soon renounced his Catholic religion and later, when Roy visited him at the reformatory, Ray stunned him by forthrightly denouncing the Bible and stating the Pope was a "big rum dum." All of Roy's arguments to the contrary failed to change his mind.

Prior to this visit with Ray, Roy had frequently given thought to entering the priesthood and had often discussed it with Father Buck, of Eugene, who had even gone so far as to make arrangements for Roy's study, without cost, in California. However, with the family in continual need of help and Ray still in the reformatory, he decided against such a course and kept working with his father at the Salem barber shop. His eyes constantly gave him trouble, eventually causing him to leave the barber shop and take a job at the State Hospital in Salem, where he earned a salary of $57.50 a month, plus room and board.

On May 12, 1921, the 21 year old Ray was released from prison, having served a full 12 months. After a year's association with experienced young criminals, he now had a cheap suit of clothes, a $5 bill, no religion, and a malevolent grudge against society for what he considered a rank injustice. He felt the world owed him something and his efforts to collect on this fancied debt ruined, not only his life and the lives of most of his family, but the lives of many other people as well. Perhaps it was merely one link in the diabolic chain of destiny pulling a tighter and tighter noose around him and those close to him.

Chapter 6

A Crime is Spawned

Following Ray's release from the reformatory, he returned to Salem, to share a second-rate room with Roy. Unable to find a job, he grew morose and more virulent. The twins held numerous intense philosophical discussions, but with Ray by far the better read, and more eloquent, Roy's religious convictions soon began to erode and he, too, became convinced of the great inequity done to Ray.

In June 1921, Ray went to Spokane, Washington, where a former cell mate at Monroe, William A. Clark, had arranged for him to work at the Brown News Co. as his helper, doing chores in the kitchen and peddling lunches to passing trains at Spokane. Ray quit after one day, saying he wasn't cut out for that kind of work. A few days later he returned to Salem, although he continued to correspond with Clark for about a year.

It appears the idea for a major crime had first begun fermenting while Ray was in the reformatory. He advised Roy he had the address of some "high-powered" criminals in Chicago, obtained from another inmate there, and he was going to join them, stating a participation in one big robbery could provide $50,000 or more. This would easily enable them all to live without such a continuous struggle. Roy volunteered to accompany him to Chicago, but the offer was refused.

Around October 1921, he "beat" his way to Chicago, on the Northern Pacific. Unable to locate the supposed crime syndicate, he returned to Salem in disgust, even more thoroughly discouraged than before. While in Chicago he had visited I.W.W. headquarters and wrote his friend Clark that he was much disappointed and that the place was a "miserable, crummy dump."

During that winter Ray, Roy and their older brother, Verne, roomed together, but it was a very difficult time for the three young men, as neither Ray or Verne were able to obtain regular employment. This, probably, was in no way a reflection on either of them, for millions of other men were out of work during the period and Oregon, in particular, was a difficult area for finding a job.

As Clark later recalled, Ray's last letter in June 1922, indicated that he was "extremely despondent and that he was considering committing suicide . . . his eyes had failed him, the "Wobbly" organization had proved disloyal to him . . . that his friends had turned against him and he had about decided to end it all."

Roy again volunteered to participate in committing a major robbery and it was so decided. A stake was needed, however, for weapons, getaway material, etc., so the two young men left Salem for Portland. They managed to find work constructing a logging road and, between them, finally saved $75 to use in launching their venture into big time crime.

In the meantime, Ray had been in contact with a former cell mate from Monroe, who claimed it would be a pushover to hold up the bank in Yacolt, Washington, a few miles northeast of Vancouver. Plans were laid and the three agreed to meet there on July 2, 1922, and hold up the small bank the following day. For some reason, the third man did not appear for the meeting, but the brothers went on to Yacolt anyway. After looking over the situation, it didn't seem to suit their objectives so they left and headed for the Oregon cost.

Robbery of the bank at Seaside was contemplated, but the proximity of the police station loomed as too large a threat and that idea was discarded. By then, all the $75 had been spent and a decision was reached to rob the general store at Cannon Beach to get enough money to live on until such time as the big strike could be made. Not wanting to be seen lurking in the vicinity, they hid out near the store to wait for night. During the long, boring day, lying concealed, the thought entered their minds of maybe killing someone during the holdup and the possibility then of becoming wanted men for only a few hundred dollars in loot. They decided against robbing the store.

The night of July 3, 1922, the date when they were to have solved all their financial worries through the robbery of the Yacolt bank, was spent sleeping out on the beach near Seaside, broke, hungry and thoroughly depressed.

Sometime later they considered the bank at Florence, but having no money for provisions or escape equipment, that thought was soon given up. Eventually, they made their way back to Salem, where Roy again returned to working in his father's shop. But, a short time later, he moved to Albany to work in a barber shop there, even though his eyes continued to plague him more and more and he could hardly see to cut hair at times. He was extremely worried about going blind.

Roy was convinced that constant barbering would cost him his eyesight and contemplated filing on a homestead somewhere on the coast. On discussing this thought with a so-called, professional land locater, one Mr. Alonzo Dole, he was assured a claim could easily be found, with plenty of nearby fishing and hunting, ample timber and spring water. The man was given a $10 deposit to find such a site. A few days later the gentleman was arrested and thrown in jail for starting fires to clear land. Roy never saw him again, nor was his money returned. Thoughts of homesteading were abandoned.

The twins spent the balance of the Summer of 1922 working at various logging camps in Oregon, using a series of aliases, including F. H. Hall (Roy) and J. H. Hall (Ray) and others. In the Fall of 1922, the youngest brother, Lee, had an argument with his father and came up to the logging camp where they were employed. He also used an alias, so it wouldn't be known he was their brother, but, unable to hire on, soon returned to Albany. *(Author's note: This continued use of aliases is not such a reflection on the character of the boys as might be assumed. Names were not too important at logging camps during that era and members of a family frequently would change their names when working in the same camp. There were no withholding taxes or social security deductions then, so names meant little. In case of strikes or special situations, a new name solved many problems quite easily.)*

That Fall, the four boys, Ray, Roy, Verne and Lee (Hugh was still in New Mexico attending high school) were together for the first time in years. Verne had worked all summer in a logging camp, saving several hundred dollars. Upon meeting his brothers, he spent around $150 on clothes for Roy, as well as buying him a watch. The boys bought young Lee his first suit, an overcoat and other clothes. *(It is interesting to note the total unselfishness of the five brothers, as they unquestioningly shared whatever they had with each other.)*

The twins had been frequently attending the 1st Christian Church in Albany. Being young, single, good looking and quite personable, they became acquainted with numerous girls in the area. Among these, was Dorothy Wiberg, with whom Roy fell in love. Just before Christmas, in 1922, Roy went from Eugene to Albany to spend some time with his girl friend, registering at the St. Francis Hotel as Howard A. Harris. During this visit, a trip was made to a nearby photo gallery and pictures were taken for her . . . the same picture that was to haunt him later from thousands of reward posters. In short order, Roy's small bankroll had vanished and he returned to stay with his father and work part time in the barber shop, which had by then moved to Eugene.

During that winter, Ray continually brooded about his inability to find employment, becoming more and more dejected and moody. Early in the Spring, he hitched a ride on a southbound freight train, making his way back to New Mexico for a short visit with his mother and Hugh. During the trip south, as he later admitted, a careful lookout was maintained for good train robbery sites and he was particularly impressed with the summit of the Siskiyou Mountains. While in New Mexico, Ray confided to Hugh the plans for a holdup, urging Hugh to join them following graduation.

At the Artesia High School, Hugh had been an outstanding student, according to "The Rattler" (1923 yearbook), captain of the basketball team, on the football team, athletic editor of "The Rattler" and president of the "A" Club. Under his class picture was the comment, "An optimist in the guise of a pessimist." His senior class picture later decorated the reward posters throughout the world and was the picture which eventually provided the tip for his capture.

Early in the Spring of 1923, Roy, accompanied by Eddy Wiberg, the 14-year old brother of his girl friend, went to work in a nearby logging camp, earning $5.60 per day. The youngster also obtained a job splitting wood for the donkey engine, earning $3.60 a day. The jobs were short-lived, however, in that a strike had been called for April 1st, and both were forced to leave.

Soon thereafter, Ray arrived back in Oregon and joined Roy, by then working at the Silver Falls Lumber Company, in Silverton. In June, following graduation, Hugh, accompanied by a young friend, Lowell Naylor, came to Oregon. Taking the name of E. E. James, he joined his two brothers at Silverton, where much time was spent discussing robbery plans and studying the techniques of other famous criminals throughout the country. Exploits of the then-famous Roy Gardner, who had obtained many thousands of dollars from train robberies, impressed them greatly. They planned to commit one big-money crime, in hopes of acquiring sufficient wealth so they'd never have to struggle again.

A strike had been called at the Silver Falls Lumber Company, to take place around September 1st, so after talking it over, the three plotters decided it was a propitious time to put their long-smoldering scheme into action. The decision was to loot a mail train, feeling this offered the greatest opportunity to obtain a lot of money at one fell swoop. Ironically, the boys were probably in the best financial and physical condition of their lives, but they had a rendezvous with malevolent destiny and could wait no longer.

On August 30, 1923, the three of them went to Portland, registering at a second-rate hotel under assumed names . . . Hugh again whimsically selecting the name of J. James, which he wrote with the tell-tale "J" so easily identifiable by the authorities when they later were searching hotel registers. A 1918 Nash touring car was purchased for around $900 from R. L. Stowall, at a Burnside Street used car lot, with 2 months payment being made in advance, and registered to Roy DeAutremont. They also bought a repeating shotgun, a supply of .22 and .45 calibre cartridges and some camping gear from a nearby store, which Hugh ordered delivered to the hotel.

Upon returning to Silverton, much of their spare time was given to target shooting . . . practicing fast, snap shooting, shooting from the hip and so forth, to familiarize themselves thoroughly with the newly purchased weapons.

A few days later they left, driving north almost to Seattle, searching for the perfect robbery site on the railroad. They couldn't seem to find the appropriate place but Ray remembered the Siskiyou Summit which had so impressed him during his freight train ride observations a few months earlier. They turned south. Near Oregon City, a Southern Pacific construction project was passed; this seemed an opportune situation and that night they sneaked back and swiped a case of dynamite, a detonating device, a roll of blasting wire and caps. All these items were placed inside Hugh's trunk in the Nash.

Stopping in Eugene, they visited with their father for a few days and, on leaving, advised him they were going on a hunting trip in the Puget Sound area. From that time until their capture in 1927, he would not again see or hear from the twins.

Roy was morbidly preoccupied with the threatening dangers which lay ahead and felt there was a great chance of not coming out of the venture alive. In view of this fatalistic outlook and a desire, in case of death, to show evidence of his love, several different insurance policies were purchased, naming his sweetheart and his older brother, Verne, as beneficiaries. Some of the policies were obtained from the Guardian Life Insurance Company of Eugene, and, in total, reached some $30,000 in face value, with $60,000 for double indemnity.

At a store along the highway, a compass was obtained, along with a map, giving details of the southern part of the state.

Driving south, they went through Roseburg, past Medford, and then on beyond Ashland, eventually arriving at the Siskiyou Summit, where the car was carefully concealed alongside a narrow mountain road.

During the next several days they walked the hills for several miles in every direction, to acquaint themselves thoroughly with the terrain. About two or three miles west of the railroad tunnel, part way down the side of Brushy Bald Mountain, an almost perfect hideout and cache was located. It was beneath a huge, fallen log which stretched across the small, nearby stream, and, while somewhat cramped in space for three men, did provide excellent concealment. This was stocked with food, first aid equipment, blankets and ammunition.

As the moment for the robbery grew closer, it was decided the car just might create complications and should be returned to Eugene and stored in their father's garage. On the morning of September 26th, 19-year old Hugh took the car from its place of hiding and left for Eugene. Driving down the mountain, he rounded a sharp curve and slammed into a cow placidly standing in the middle of the road.

The front end of the car was badly damaged, but Hugh managed to get into Ashland, where he took it to the Park Garage for repair. John McCracken was the mechanic and later testified at the trial, identifying Hugh as the person who brought in the damaged auto.

It took three days for the car to be fixed, with Hugh nervously moving daily to a new rooming house, registering each time as E. E. James. Finally, on the 29th of September the car was repaired and he hurriedly left for Eugene, arriving there in the middle of the night, with the family all in bed. He told them the camping trip had been a real mess, with almost continual rain, and that their camp outfit, including the tarpaulin loaned them by their father, had been set afire and destroyed while they were away. Hugh advised he had taken the twins back to the Silverton lumber camp. Leaving the car in his father's garage, he departed the following morning, ostensibly for Silverton. He too, would not again be seen by the family until in custody of the authorities in 1927.

Hugh had promised to mail the insurance policy receipts to Roy's girl friend, Dorothy, but, in all the confusion, this was forgotten, and then, later, when he remembered, her address had been lost so he couldn't mail them.

Buying a train ticket to Ashland, he anxiously hurried back to where his brothers were worriedly awaiting his return. Planning to hitch a ride from Ashland to the top of the Siskiyous, he was hanging around the train yard when the suspicions of a Southern Pacific special agent were aroused. On being detained and searched, Roy's insurance receipts, a roll of friction tape, flashlight batteries and bulbs were found. While Hugh told a rambling story of being on his way to San Francisco, his lack of luggage and evasive answers were not sufficient to settle the agent's suspicions. However, after lengthy questioning, the agent took the appropriate amount of money from Hugh's billfold, leaving only some small change, and obligingly purchased him a ticket to San Francisco.

Seemingly waiting for the next passenger train south, he managed to give the watchful special agents the slip and hiked from Ashland to the cabin on the far side of the mountain, arriving the following morning, October 9, 1923. Very downcast in spirit, he told what had happened, of the car repair clues probably left behind, and that the special agents now had his name and also Roy's with proof of their being in the vicinity immediately prior to the time of the robbery. He felt quick identification through his series of mishaps would be inevitable.

Despite all the potentially adverse circumstances, the decision was made to proceed with the undertaking as originally planned. Ray's morale was also at a new, low ebb, he was completely willing to gamble his life on the small prospect of success in the crime. Roy was certain he would be totally blind within another year or two, so cared little either way. Both were convinced the future offered them nothing without considerable money. *(Author's note: It does appear from later interviews and comments by all three that their motives were actually only to get money to help their family and eliminate some of their continuous hardships. There was apparently never a thought of a life of crime or high living. Money was needed for medical treatment of their youngest brother, and their mother and father were both in constant need.)*

Roy wanted to ask his sweetheart to marry him, but being in such poor financial straits, with a future clouded by potential blindness, felt this was impossible. 19-year-old Hugh, dazzled by the companionship of his older brothers and out on his own for the first time, was totally under their influence and agreeable to whatever course they selected.

They had almost no money left, but the entire operation had been thoroughly planned, with escape equipment and a stock of supplies. It was agreed everything would be gambled on this one massive effort to get rich quick. Next day all surplus material was gathered and burned. Their shoes were soaked in creosote, to prevent trailing by bloodhounds. And the following morning, carrying knapsacks, guns, flashlights, wire, the detonating machine wrapped in an old pair of Roy's overalls, a pound can of black pepper and a suitcase filled with dynamite, they headed for the west exit of tunnel #13.

After concealing the equipment near the tunnel, they sprinkled the black pepper around the area. Dusky grease paint was smeared on their faces to prevent any easy remembrance of features, or if seen, to give the impression they were merely Mexican section hands. Roy and Hugh stuck the .45 pistols in their belts and began walking through the long tunnel toward the east entrance. Ray hunkered down behind some brush on the nearby hillside.

It was just before 1:00 p.m., October 11, 1923, and the first section of train #13 was rumbling slowly away from the quick stop at Siskiyou Station toward the 3,000-foot tunnel, a short distance ahead.

Chapter 7

A Crime is Committed

For several weeks prior to the crimes, the three young brothers had holed up in the remote cabin on the Siskiyous, checking on the time schedule of train No. 13, the so-called "Gold Express", and choosing a day when they felt the valuable mail would be the heaviest. Their food cache and hideout had been prepared. They were now ready to rob train # 13.

Armed with the repeating shotgun and a .45 pistol, Ray squatted behind some bushes near the west exit, nervously smoking cigarettes; Hugh and Roy were beyond the 3,000 foot tunnel, crouched behind some brushy shrubs on the flank of the mountain, awaiting arrival of the ill-fated train. Each had a .45 Colt automatic in his belt, and Roy had a blackjack in his pocket, as well.

Hidden alongside the tunnel, tensely, they waited. The train slowed to a stop at the Siskiyou Station; after a few minutes, the high-ball whistle pierced the mountain air and slowly it rumbled up the track to a rendezvous with destiny and railroad history.

A few hundred feet from the tunnel, the engineer tested the brakes, slowing the train to a snail's pace. Then, just before reaching the tunnel entrance, it began gathering speed. The two young men darted from their concealment alongside the tracks. Hugh was in the lead and quickly swung aboard. Roy was running behind, trying to grab the hand-hold, when his pistol slipped from his waist, clattering along the track causing him to pause for a few seconds. However, there wasn't time to stop and pick it up, and, anyway, the identifying serial numbers had been filed off, so he didn't retrieve it. The momentary delay did cause trouble though, in that he couldn't reach the hand-hold and was starting to drop back as the train gained speed. Realizing the trouble, Hugh quickly stretched his leg back so Roy could grab the toe of his shoe and pull himself forward to grab the iron bar. And, even though Roy had lost his gun, there was still the blackjack.

They thought the engineer and fireman might have seen them but the Mexican section crew didn't seem to pay any attention — apparently, just two more hobos grabbing a free ride to somewhere — wherever hobos grabbed free rides to.

As the train entered the tunnel, they clambered over the tender and Hugh shoved the big .45 at the engineer, telling him to stop the train, with the engine just clear of the tunnel, and if he did not do so, they would kill him. The engineer looked as though he was going to laugh at someone's idea of a practical joke but, nevertheless, obeyed the command and the engine ground slowly to a halt, just outside the tunnel exit.

As Hugh and Roy ordered the engineer and fireman from the cab and to the front of the engine, away from the mail car, Ray ran forward with the shotgun cradled in his arms. Roy complained that his pistol had been lost and was quickly handed the one from Ray's belt.

The door on the express car noisily slid open and the mail clerk querulously peered out to see what was causing the delay; almost by reflex, Ray yanked the trigger on the shotgun, sprinkling the side of the car with rattling buckshot; the clerk jerked his head inside, apparently escaping unscathed, and slammed the door shut. His respite was only momentary, for, after a few hurried yells to open up, with no response from inside, Ray ran for the suitcase of dynamite which had been hidden near the bank. He handed it to Roy, who laid it at the front of the mail car, with the few extra sticks piled on top. Farther back, in the baggage car, Hugh Haffey also wondered at the unscheduled stop and slid open the door to find out what was going on. Stunned at the sight of several men with guns pointed at the engine crew, he quietly closed and locked the door.

Originally, the plan was to have Ray detonate the blast, as he was somewhat more experienced in the use of explosives, however, in the excitement, Roy dashed to the detonator and shoved the plunger down, raising a blinding cloud of dust and smoke from the tunnel, with scalding steam spewing from punctured pipes on the train. . .all from a huge overcharge of dynamite. The blast reverberated from mountainside to mountainside; the engine's bell tolled its doleful dirge; and the die was irretrievably cast. There was no long any chance to turn back.

Hugh ordered the shaken engineer and fireman back into the cab, preparatory to pulling the mail car out of the tunnel, while Ray and Roy examined the interior of the ripped-open car. Roy finally ran to the rear and was struggling to uncouple it when he saw an approaching red light and an unsuspecting brakeman. The astonished brakeman, suddenly confronted with a pistol, was told his life was in great danger, as a robbery was in progress, and to help uncouple the train. He advised the car had to be moved forward at the same time the pin was lifted. Reluctant to leave the brakeman by himself, Roy ordered him to raise his hands and go tell the fellows at the engine to pull the train forward.

As the brakeman slowly advanced through the smoke and dust, he apparently forgot about keeping his hands in the air and, when he and his red light suddenly emerged from the murkiness, the two startled brothers jumped to the conclusion he must have killed Roy. Ray whirled and blasted him with the shotgun, at the same instant Hugh shot him with the pistol. Slowly crumpling to the ground, riddled with buckshot, he mumbled, "That other fellow said to pull the thing ahead."

Everything was going wrong for the DeAutremonts. They couldn't get into the mail car where the valuables were, due to the heavy smoke and burning debris. The blast had lifted the car wheels off the track and, despite the efforts of the engineer, it couldn't be moved. Panic began to set in as they suddenly realized the whole thing was turning into a big fiasco, with no treasure forthcoming. In sheer, frightened, angry frustration, Roy jabbed his pistol at the unsuspecting fireman, numbly standing with his hands in the air alongside the engine, and pulled the trigger. Now, two men were sprawled by the engine and another in the mail car, all dead or dying. Unknown to the holdup men, the expressman laid in the express car, unconscious from the tremendous concussion of the blast.

Ray and Roy again scrambled into the mail car, in a last desperate effort to salvage some of the valuables therein, but the biting smoke from the overturned stove and burning mailsacks was even worse, boiling through the confined space, punctuated with hissing streams of scalding steam. They could not reach the mail sacks. Glaring at the smoking, fiery mess, they realized it would be impossible to get to anything of value for an hour or more and it would be just too dangerous to hang around any longer. Jumping down, one of them, realizing the frightened engineer had been a witness to the entire bloody event, growled at Hugh, still guarding the engineer in the cab, "Bump him off and come on." Shoving his gun to the terrified man's head, Hugh yanked the trigger and suddenly four men were dead or dying.

Bitterly, they realized their violent quest for quick and easy riches had been totally fruitless.

Having no loot to carry from the scene, there was no longer any need for the three knapsacks lying beside the tracks. Breaking into a panicked run, they fled up the hill away from their murderous debacle in crime.

The engine bell continued its monotonous clanging, the sound pursuing them, fainter and fainter, until it too, faded into nothing, as had their dream of wealth.

On reaching the crest of a nearby ridge, Hugh and Roy began arguing as to which was the correct route to the hideout. Finally, Roy gave in and they hurried off across the hill. Before long though, all agreed it was the wrong direction, with Roy then taking over the chore of finding the right trail. After retracing their way for a mile or two, the right route was found. Late that afternoon, airplanes could be seen and heard flying back and forth over the mountains and the boys realized they were the subjects of an aerial search. It was almost dusk by the time they wearily crawled into hiding, to lie there exhausted from their flight and sheer nervous despair.

In the original plans, Ray was to have gone to Eugene, following the robbery, to pickup the Nash get-away car stored at their father's home. Due to the problems created by Hugh's wrecking the car and the subsequent clues he probably left, including being questioned by railroad inspectors on returning through Ashland, they decided against following that plan.

Their hideout was located about 2 or 3 miles west of the west tunnel exit, on the side of Brushy Bald Mountain and carefully fashioned beneath an old log. The nearby creek enabled them to get water without leaving their place of concealment. That it was a good site is born out of the fact that to anyone's knowledge, it has never been found. There, for the following twelve or thirteen days, the brothers holed up. While the place was stocked with food, first aid material and extra ammunition, it was very confining with only limited space for moving about.

When the food supply began to dwindle, Ray decided to try and get to Eugene and pick up the car if things weren't too hot. Taking the pistol back from Roy, he hooked a ride at the west end of the tunnel on a northbound freight train. The DeAutremonts must have had extremely loose waists for their bad luck in hanging on to pistols was phenomenal. Their second pistol was dropped by Ray as he grabbed the fast moving train.

Outside of Medford, he quickly slipped off the train and strolled casually into town and to a restaurant. Picking up a newspaper, he was stunned to discover his own face and that of his twin brother Roy staring back at him, captioned "Have you seen the DeAutremont twins?" Nervously, he left the restaurant and walked around town, anticipating arrest at any moment. There were posters everywhere with the faces of the brothers prominently displayed — and a reward of $14,400 for them, dead or alive. Everyone was talking about the crime and, obviously, going to Eugene for the car was totally out of the question.

With but little money, a job was a necessity, so he walked towards Central Point and then turned towards the little town of Jacksonville, some 5 miles to the west. There he obtained a job picking apples for Mr. C.C. Hoover *(there is some disagreement as to whether he picked pears or apples, but Mr. Hoover said it was apples)*. Ironically, board and room were arranged for with a Mr. Dave Finley, who was extremely active with the local posses searching for the suspects and spent much of his time hunting them. Each day the intrepid Mr. Finley would buckle on his gun belt, put on his heavy sheepskin coat and hie off to the mountains looking for the killers. Mrs. Finley would surely have fainted dead away had she realized one of the murderers was sleeping and eating in her home. Even in his threatened straits, the humor of the situation touched Ray. *(Some accounts show Ray as working for Finley)*.

As soon as he was able to accumulate a few dollars, Ray bought a supply of raisins and other easy to carry food items. That night he sneaked onto a southbound freight train and made his way back to the mountain where, in the darkness, he floundered from the tunnel, through the woods and across the hillsides to the hideout. He gave his brothers the few goodies he had brought and related the bleak news.

He revealed that there was a $4,800 reward on each of them, dead or alive, and all the talk was of catching and hanging them; that hundreds of armed men were combing the mountains in search of them. Ray was in a complete state of despondency and glumly stated, "Life has dealt me its last dirty blow . . . I'm going to be leaving you", intimating he was going to commit suicide. However, Roy persuaded him into making a fighting run for it, with Hugh numbly agreeing to go along with whatever they decided.

After considering all alternatives, they decided to pack the little food which was still left, Hugh's .45 pistol and the shotgun, what shells they could carry, along with their bedrolls, and in a desperate effort to escape, strike out through the rugged mountains for the coast.

For pure, dumb luck in evading capture, the following three and a half years offer an absolutely astonishing example.

The objects of a massive man hunt by practically every single law enforcement agency in the U.S., they miraculously stumbled through and around thousands of pursuing officers, as well as untold numbers of amateur detectives trying to win the reward money.

It seems impossible that they were not apprehended sooner, but perhaps it was another fickle flick of fate to let them each have a sweet taste of the good life which might have been. Then, almost like grabbing candy from a child, everything was snatched from them, never to be returned.

Chapter 8

They Try to Escape

Early on the morning of October 29th, the fugitives crawled from their log hideout and headed west. For the next three days, using their compass, they cautiously walked in the direction of the coast, keeping an eye cocked for the airplanes which still occasionally cruised low overhead. Open ridges were carefully avoided and they were ever watchful for posse members still ranging through the mountains. Tracks of searchers were all over the place and at night camp fires were frequently seen burning . . . markers of the searching parties.

Food was very short and the strain soon began to tell as they weakened from their daily hardships and shortage of nourishment. At night they slept huddled in their bedrolls beneath the bushes.

On the fourth day menacing clouds closed in and it began to snow. Just about that same moment an isolated, uninhabited cabin was reached. Searching inside, they found a container of dry beans which gave their spirits an inspiring lift, and they proceeded to cook them. After boiling the beans for 3 or 4 hours, they wolfed down the half-cooked hot meal, the first they had had in days. It was their most comfortable night since leaving the Mt. Crest cabin, almost a month earlier. Warmed by the fireplace and with bellies full of hot food, they slept through the night. For breakfast, they finished the pot of beans.

A number of small logging operations were in the area and they had to be extremely careful to avoid these but they continued to slant in a westerly direction, struggling through falling snow most of the day. Two separate times on that fifth day, deer were sighted and quickly shot at, but both were missed. By the evening of that day, strong doubts began to arise as to the possibility of reaching the coast at that time of the year. The food was nearly gone and the increasing depth of snow made progress more and more difficult. Many tortuous miles of steep, snow-clad, rugged, brush-covered country still lay between them and the coast, and winter was in full swing.

Stumbling out of the brush, onto a logging road, the trio sat down to discuss the worsening situation. Staring at the snow-covered

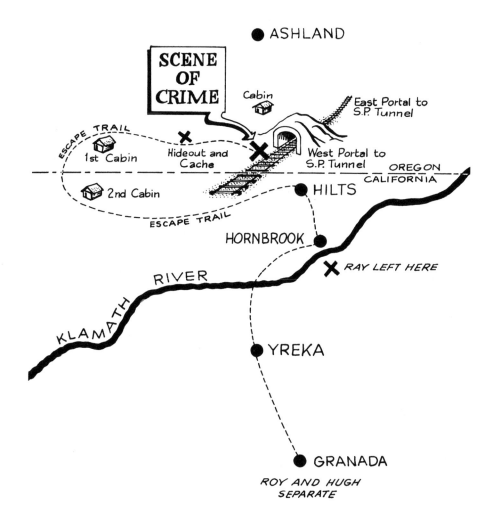

wilderness facing them, it was decided to give up traveling west and turn and follow the logging road, hopeful of finding something to eat. All three were almost totally exhausted from lack of food, the strenuous activity and continuous exposure to the worsening winter weather. Most of the cartridges had been thrown away to lighten their load and, finally, even the blanket rolls were discarded as they struggled to keep going.

The following day another deserted cabin was found, although it was all too close to several inhabited houses for any great peace of mind. It was biting cold and to keep warm a fire was built in the fireplace which gave them a moment of considerable concern when a man walked by and stopped for awhile, peering at the swirl of smoke rising from the chimney — but, after a long look, he passed on. An abandoned vegetable patch was sighted near the cabin and they slipped out to investigate. To their gratification, some lettuce, turnips and onions remained, which they gathered. These were hungrily devoured raw as they sprawled in front of the blazing fire. Then, utterly exhausted, they slept in the warm cabin until evening.

At dusk, they sneaked out of the cabin and down the logging road, past the other houses, in the general direction of Hilts. During the night a logging camp was passed and Ray and Hugh broke into the commissary, stealing a slab of bacon and a hind quarter of veal. All were so hungry, at that point, that they sliced off chunks of bacon and ate them raw. Later, they crawled into a bushy area alongside the logging road and roasted some of the meat. It was a most welcome feast, but they were still very weak from hunger and very, very weary.

By the seventh day they were nearing the little town of Hilts and it was expected they could get there by the following evening. However, when still a short distance away, the weather became absolutely abominable, raining and snowing, with periodic showers of sleet to add to the fugitives' misery. It was a horrible time to be out in the open, and finally they could tolerate it no longer, slipping into the sheltering woods, where a big fire was built. Huddling around the warming fire, they roasted more of the stolen meat.

On the night of the eighth day, they finally reached the outskirts of Hilts and were walking along towards the train yard when car lights suddenly shone on them and followed slowly for a short way. While near panic and certain they had been discovered, they resignedly kept walking towards the yard and depot, until, at last, the car turned off and drove away.

There was another extremely close squeak at Hilts, when a few hundred yards farther down the track, the Hilts police saw them and yelled at them to stop. The threesome ignored the command and the police started after them. Roy no longer had a gun, so he went on ahead, down the tracks, with Hugh (who still had his pistol) following, and Ray, with the shotgun concealed under his overcoat, bringing up behind. The brothers soon slipped off to one side of the track and into the nearby bushes. At this, the officers turned back, without further pursuit, probably assuming they were merely three wandering hobos.

That night they located a bit of shelter in a drain, a short way south of Hilts, where a small fire was made and most of the remaining meat roasted and eaten. It was another numbingly cold night, and even though huddled near the fire trying to keep warm, the raw, bone-chilling wind still cut through their damp clothing, adding tremendously to their abject misery. It was difficult to find any firewood and exploding sparks from the damp limbs would periodically land on their clothing to arouse them from a sleepy stupor with the stench of scorched cloth.

The brothers were extremely despondent, certain the Hilts' police would be notifying authorities in Hornbrook and elsewhere of their presence in the area and that their desperate flight to freedom was about to come to an end. The shotgun was abandoned here as they felt it would be overly conspicuous in these more populated areas, and anyway they were tired of lugging it along.

Towards the next evening, they came out of hiding, hoping to slip through Hornbrook that night. Concerned by the number of vehicles coming and going along the highway, they were very cautious, but no one seemed to pay any attention to them, even when they made a small fire and ate all but a tiny portion of the meat.

Hornbrook was reached later that evening and Ray, who had shaved and trimmed his hair earlier in the day (even though they had thrown away their blankets, they still carried barber's tools) took all their cash - a total of 15 cents - and strolled downtown to a confectionery store where he bought three candy bars. While in the store, he listened with great interest to the men there, still talking about the terrible train robbery and how "they will get them."

Slowly the fugitives proceeded on past Hornbrook, following the road until about midnight, when they came to the Klamath River. There, a fire was build in a sheltered pocket in the rocks by the river bank, and through the rest of the long night they hunched over it striving to keep warm, periodically dozing for a moment until the piercing cold bit at their bones, for there was no longer even a blanket to wrap around them to ward off the frigid November winds whipping along the river.

Next morning, the decision was made to split up, for to continue as a trio through areas where people would be frequently encountered had to be more than foolhardy. A number of intricate schemes were agreed upon for making certain of future contact by letter and the use of various aliases. In thirty days they were to write each other, using the aliases of Johnie Johnson (Roy), William

R. Elliott (Ray) and James C. Price (Hugh). If, for some reason, connections were not made by these means, they agreed to meet in New York City on New Year's Day 1928, at the biggest YMCA, or to leave a notice at some prominent place in various New York libraries.

Chapter 9

The Fugitives Separate

When the boys parted that bleak November morning beside the Klamath River, they shook hands. Sunken eyes, drawn features and dirty, shabby clothing recorded their grave trials of the preceding weeks. There wasn't a solitary dime among them . . . and thousands of people were searching for them, anxious to shoot them on sight. Good-byes were said, not knowing when, if ever, they would be together or if they would even lay eyes on each other again. Ray slowly walked away first, on down the road without ever looking back.

Roy and Hugh sat glumly by the river for another hour or so, then they too, started down the road. Late in the afternoon they came to a place along the river where some fellows were spearing salmon. Roy strolled down to them and, after striking up a conversation, was given one of the fish.

They continued walking down the highway, carrying the fish, when a man stopped his car and offered them a ride into Yreka. They really didn't want to pass through the town but couldn't reasonably refuse the lift without creating suspicion, so calmly rode with him into the center of town. Still carrying the salmon by its gills, they slowly walked through the business district, sure of recognition at every step. By this time though, they were downright disreputable looking and a far cry from the dapper individuals so carefully described on the reward posters. Their shoes were worn out and the clothing they had been wearing, day and night, since the attempted robbery, was in tatters from encounters with brush and night-time huddling around spark-spitting camp fires.

Continuing on past Yreka, they reached an abandoned road-gang camp, where a syrup bucket was found, still containing quite a bit of syrup. Roy went to a nearby house to bum some food and was given a few cold biscuits. Another hobo was also at the camp and generously shared his coffee with them. These, plus the roasted salmon, provided the first really all-they-could-eat meal since the early days in the mountain hideout, except for the pot of half-cooked beans at the abandoned cabin.

Enduring another night of misery, they tried to doze near the camp fire. The freezing winter wind whipped bitingly through their worn clothing and it was difficult to obtain enough wood to keep the fire going. When dawn finally arrived, they finished the fish, drank the rest of the coffee and trudged along towards Weed.

Near the tiny town of Grenada, a hay field was passed where a farmer was working. Roy called to him, asking if a hired hand was needed. The farmer, named Bill Johns, offered to hire both of them but Roy quickly whispered to Hugh that only one of them should work there. Hugh decided he'd rather go on.

Afraid even to shake hands within the view of the farmer, the brothers just whispered a painful goodbye, not to see or hear from each other again until June 21, 1927, when both were in jail at Jacksonville, Oregon. *(These details are somewhat at variance with other accounts but this is the way Roy delated it in his confession and therefore this version of the separation is given.)*

When asked his name, Roy came up with that of a former school mate — Clarence H. Dodgeworth — which, as he later stated in his confession, was the most innocuous name he'd ever heard of. Roy worked for the farmer until mid-December, learning to cope with many of the problems he was to face regularly until captured. Continually, it was necessary to be on the alert to prevent a slip of the tongue which might betray him; to respond to another name. Almost daily there were conversations regarding the DeAutremonts, what fiends they must be, and on and on . . . once the farmer asked Roy if the fellow who had been with him when asking for work was his brother. While his heart was in his mouth, Roy nonchalantly replied he was only some bum he had just met that day.

The Johns family were members of the Mormon Church in Grenada and frequently Roy was pursuaded to attend services with them. One wonders what the congregation's reaction would have been had they realized the identity of the quiet young man in their midst who sang the hymns so well.

On leaving the employment of Mr. Johns, Roy apparently had a little trouble obtaining his pay. But, through a bit of subterfuge, he induced the farmer to give him a check, which was cashed in Grenada where he bought $10 worth of clothing. Again, one ponders on the thoughts of Bill Johns when he learned the young hired hand with whom he had argued about pay had been one of the bloody DeAutremonts. *(It has been stated that Roy stole money from the farmer, but, again, not according to his written confession and description of the occasion.)*

Roy planned to buy a ticket on the passenger train going through Grenada around 3 a.m. but, it was a foggy night, and apparently the engineer didn't see him, for the train didn't stop on his signal. So, at daylight, he again began hiking down the Pacific Highway.

After much walking and some periodic hitchhiking, he arrived at Redding. He made a tour of the employment agencies but was unable to find any work and went on to Sacramento. There, using the name of Charley Johnson, he rented a housekeeping room at the Bachelor's Hotel.

Roy was still not very sturdy and had trouble finding work. Finally, when down to his last $1.50, a job was found near Sacramento, pruning grapes. After only two days, he was fired for not working fast enough.

Again, like a migrating wild goose with but a single thought in mind, he slanted toward the south, continuing down the Pacific Highway. *(Where were all the police during this period, while the three young fugitives were openly making their way along the highway?)*

A friendly fellow, on his way to Vacaville, gave him a ride and suggested it would be an excellent place to try for a job. Roy took the man's advice and, near Vacaville, obtained work at the Uhl ranch, with pay of $2.50 per day. While there, he used the name of Johnny Johnson and boarded himself.

In accordance with their prearranged plans, Roy wrote letters to both Ray and Hugh, and if the Postmaster or postal clerks at the post office had been alert, the whole case would have been over right then, for Roy's letter to Ray was addressed to William R. Elliott, one of the aliases listed prominently on the reward posters tacked to the lobby wall of the post office.

Hugh did not receive either Roy or Ray's letters but Ray did get Roy's letter and, shortly thereafter, Roy had a letter from Ray, who was then using the name of Carlson. Following an exchange of several letters, in May 1924, the twins arranged to meet at night in Vacaville. Despite all their problems, it was a joyful reunion. The twins were very close, and, when parting months before, both had been tired, ragged, hungry and desperate. Now they were well clothed, well fed and in excellent physical condition.

Talking far into the night, they wondered what had happened to Hugh, but, as no publicity had been seen regarding his capture, felt certain he, too, was still safely at large. However, the continuing threat of identification hung menacingly over their heads and each entry into a post office was traumatic — always seeing their own faces and those of their brother bleakly staring from the wall.

After thoroughly dissecting the situation, it was decided the best opportunity for escape lay in going east, farther away from the scene of the crime, and have a try at making new lives for themselves in one of the more highly populated and industrialized areas. Not wanting to travel together, in June 1924, using the alias of Jimmy Williams, Ray took the train east, eventually reaching Detroit, where he found work at an iron foundry. Roy continued to work in Vacaville, saving every dollar possible to pay his fare east.

While this was slow going on $2.50 per day, Ray assisted by sending money from time to time until December 1924, when Roy had accumulated sufficient money for the train trip.

After leaving Hilts, neither of the twins had a weapon. Roy felt he should have one and persuaded a fellow worker to buy him a mail-order Luger pistol, which he kept until his arrest at Steubenville, Ohio, in 1927. On his trip east, during a short train stop in Ogden, Utah, he was strolling near the depot and, spotting another Luger in a pawn shop, bought it for $12, for Ray.

In passing through Denver, Roy had a harrowing experience, for as he left the train it was necessary to go through a double line of police officers, who were examing each passenger. He did not know if this was because he had been reported as being on the train or not, but his experiences during the previous months stood him in good stead. Knowing he would be in big trouble if stopped and searched, having two Luger pistols with him, he strode casually past the officers, nonchalantly swinging his grip.

In Chicago, he transferred to the train for Detroit, arriving there during December 1924, and registering at the Roosevelt Hotel. The next morning he telephoned Ray, who met him in front of the hotel, and the twins were together again. Outside of being separated while working at nearby jobs, they remained together until captured.

Chapter 10

Ray and Roy Reunited

Using the name of Johnny Williams, Roy began searching for work, and almost immediately had a narrow escape when the dark glasses he was wearing attracted the attention of a detective. Noticing the detective's suspicious interest, Roy managed to elude him but it indicated the continual need for staying on the alert, every single moment. Colored glasses were common at the time in California but only drew unwanted notice in Detroit.

He soon found a dish-washing job at a hotel in South Alliance, some thirty or forty miles from Detroit. However, about two weeks after going to work, a wanted bulletin was posted at the hotel, which resulted in another resident commenting about all the detectives suddenly appearing around the hotel and wondering who they were after. This observation alarmed Roy and he immediately assumed they knew who he was and were waiting to be led to Ray and Hugh. He didn't know just what to do, but a day or so later, he was fired and quietly slipped away, returning to Detroit, where he apprehensively explained the situation to Ray.

Jumping to the conclusion that the chase must be closing in on them they contemplated flight to Canada. However, considering that circulars would be widely distributed at the border, they decided it would be better to make their way to an isolated island Ray had read about, off the coast of North Carolina, called Ocracoke Island.

Putting on what clothing could be inconspicuously worn and carrying what they could without appearing obvious, they casually walked away from Ray's quarters and left town, not even stopping to pick up Ray's pay from the plant where he worked. Moving south and east, they rode freight trains and walked until they reached Wellston, Ohio. There, in talking with other fellows on the freight trains, they learned West Virginia could be a tough state for hobos to cross, the police arresting them on the slightest pretext. In view of this, on reaching Ironton, almost on the border between Ohio, Kentucky and West Virginia, they took to the hills, living in a small abandoned cabin they found there.

The two obtained a little work cutting railroad ties for the Culbertson Lumber Company, which also provided some small shacks for its workers, enabling them to scrape through the winter, as their requirements were limited. A few months later, when they felt things had probably quieted down somewhat, they moved to Sulphur Springs. Meanwhile Roy had grown a mustache, had bleached his hair, and was going by the name of Clarence Goodwin. On the morning he came to work with light hair when it had been dark before, he took some kidding whereupon he commented, "If you had as much to worry you as I have, your hair would turn white too." Ray also had bleached his hair with peroxide and was using the name of Elmer Goodwin. They told people Arkansas was their home state and those who became acquainted with them referred to them as the "Arkansas Boys."

In May, 1925, they were working in the woods, near Ironton, and living in another mountain cabin, which had been fixed up very neatly and sported a backyard garden. At about this time, they met James Sprouse, a timber cruiser, who had a small farm nearby, along with 12 children, including 7 girls. He was much taken with the two boys and, that night, told his family he was going to invite them to supper sometime, stating, "They're smart . . . lots smarter than any of the fellows around here, and so sensible."

The following Sunday, Ray did come to supper and greatly impressed the entire family with his easy discussion of books, farming, labor problems and so forth. In talking about the garden the boys has planted, Mr. Sprouse offered to get some special seeds and Ray promised to return in a few days to get them. Later, 16-year old Hazel suggested he come out in the yard and join her and the younger children in their games.

After Ray (Elmer Goodwin) left, Mr. Sprouse said to his oldest daughter, "Hazel, that's the kind of man I want you to marry. You're a fool if you let him go; he's got brains, he's a hard worker, he's got a good education and he'll be good to you."

From then on, Ray visited the family two or three times a week, and, while Hazel was somewhat embarrassed when the other kids teased about his white hair, it didn't seem to bother him, so she didn't worry about it. The whole family was highly entertained by his jokes, songs, recitation of poetry and vast knowledge.

The boys felt it might be a good thing if one of them did get married, so they would appear to be a more stable part of the community. Following a four-month courtship of Hazel and to the joy of her parents, the marriage took place in August 1925 at nearby Greenup, Kentucky (which did not require a birth certificate or waiting period). The bride was 16 years old. Everyone told her how lucky she was to get such a nice young husband and commented how smart the "Arkansas Boys" were, except for one neighbor woman who must have had some intuition about things being too good to be true, for she said to the girl, "Hazel, I know folks are crazy about these boys, and you love Elmer, but remember, they came here from a far way off . . . maybe they're in some sort of trouble."

After the wedding, the young couple moved into a little four-room house, near her parents' farm in Pine Grove. Roy continued living at the cabin for a short time but soon moved in with Ray and Hazel. During the evenings the three young people had great fun entertaining themselves by putting on shows, and reciting poetry. Ray was very fond of Robert Services's writing and would quote "The Spell of the Yukon," "The Shooting of Dan McGrew." "Cremation of Sam McGee," etc., and the tiny house often rang to their singing of "Bringing in the Sheaves," "Farewell to Thee," and so forth. Frequently, they danced to rollicking tunes played on their dilapidated old phonograph. It was probably one of the happiest periods in the entire lives of the twins, despite the ominous possibility of capture constantly hanging over their heads. Surely, during his many years in prison, Ray must frequently have reflected on this tiny segment of his life, until the bright memory of those happy months gradually diminished into a faded, sad recollection.

In the winter of 1925/1926, Ray and Hazel went to Portsmouth to work, and later to nearby Washington. Roy stayed that winter at Pine Grove, although in the Spring of 1926 he left to work in the West Virginia coal mines, returning in midsummer to stay with Ray and Hazel, who were again living at Pine Grove.

On April 15, 1926, Elmer Goodwin applied for a job as Fire Warden for the Ohio State Forest. He gave his address as Route # 1, Box 187, Hanging Rock, Ohio, and was recommended by James Sprouse. However, he did not get the job.

On June 15, 1926 the young couple's baby was born. According to Roy, it arrived a little faster than the prospective parents had anticipated, resulting in Ray handling the delivery and providing the baby's first bath. Another source states that the baby was delivered at home by Dr. W.L. Griffith. In any event, during Hazel's confinement, Ray cooked the meals and Roy took care of the house. In naming the infant, Ray indicated a strong preference for the name of Jackie Hugh and, while the girl-mother didn't understand the reason, she agreed to it.

The boys frequently went to the Briggs Library in nearby Ironton, but one day Roy thought the librarians had recognized him and he crawled out a back window, never to go there again. Oddly enough, Miss Helen Cloran and Miss Darline Stewart had noted the circulars and had commented on the resemblance of the boys to the pictures but dismissed the matter as being totally absurd.

The personable young men continued to make friends in the area and were able to work fairly steadily. That Fall, both went to work nearby at the Hanging Rock Iron Company, tearing down a furnace stack. Ray had the reputation of being an expert with dynamite and was described as a good worker and well liked. Roy was not as good a worker and about mid-October in 1926 was fired by W.M. Jefferys, general manager, for being sullen, always complaining and a poor workman. Jefferys physically threw him out of the office after Roy cursed him. Roy again returned to West Virginia and went to work in a coal mine at McKeevy. At Christmas, he returned to spend the holidays with Ray and his family.

Although there was one occasion when Roy became drunk while playing blackjack in a moonshiner's cabin near Pine Grove and bragged about being wanted by the law for murder, nothing came of it. And, through the months and years, with their further involvement in new identities and acceptance within their remote communities, the twins were gradually becoming lulled into the faint hope that maybe the far-reaching man hunt had been evaded. There were the ever-present wanted posters but these contained pictures taken several years earlier. They were, however, extremely careful not to attract the attention of law enforcement authorities. While it seemed almost impossible, their hopes did soar from time to time. Christmas in 1926 was a most happy time for the young parents and Roy.

Following New Year's, 1927, Roy rode north with friends to Steubenville, going to work there in the coal mine operated by The Wheeling Steel Corp. When Ray learned of the good wages being paid and, now feeling more secure from their relationships in the area, he decided to join Roy. In March 1927, he moved to Steubenville, going to work for the same company.

Around mid-April, 1927, things were a little slack at the mine and Roy returned to Pine Grove for a short vacation and to visit with friends there. At Hanging Rock, he noticed a brand-new type of wanted circular had been posted, containing only the pictures of himself and Ray. *(This is questionable, for at that time the posters still contained all three pictures, but Hugh's picture was over-printed with the statement that, "Hugh DeAutremont has been apprehended. Roy and Ray are still at large.")* In any event, while Roy later stated that he had been unable to examine the poster closely, to ascertain if Hugh had been captured, something about it did thoroughly frighten him. He cut his vacation short, hurriedly returning into Steubenville to share his apprehensions with Ray. Their new-found confidence was suddenly shattered.

Although neither had seen anything in the newspapers or magazines about Hugh's capture, the answer seemed obvious and, after discussing this discouraging new development, flight to Mexico was planned. Initially, Ray had thought of marrying, primarily to assist in building a new identity, but had since fallen deeply in love with his young wife and insisted on taking her and the baby with him. This, of course, complicated matters considerably, as much more money would be needed than they had on hand. The decision was made to work another couple of months, which would give them a bank roll of around $700. Both could speak fluent Spanish, learned from their New Mexico days, and felt there would be no great problem in getting along, if they could get to Mexico safely.

They had a narrow escape a few weeks prior to their capture, when the car in which they were riding was stopped by federal prohibition agents and searched for liquor but, having none, they were released.

Roy was anxious to get transferred from the mine to the mill, where the work was somewhat more regular, a little easier and the pay better. One day about noon a fellow told him to see the employment office about a change. As he entered the office, one of the clerks glanced at him and then went on out the door. A few minutes later, the Chief of Police and two other officers came through the doors and, while Roy immediately suspected their objective, he had no place to go and tried to bluff his way through the situation. Upon being questioned, he admited being Clarence Goodwin and was arrested, handcuffed and taken to jail. After trapping himself with several conflicting statements, he admitted Elmer Goodwin was his brother.

Ray was working at night and slept days until about 3:30 p.m. A man, stating he was a claims agent, came to his door, told Hazel that Roy had been hurt in an auto accident, and asked for Ray to come with him to the doctor's office. As Ray reached the foot of the stairs, Edward Pomeroy, a special agent for the Department of Justice, stepped behind him and, outside, he noticed detectives by a car. He realized the long run was over. A couple of hours later the twins joined each other in jail. Ray had $250 cash in his pocket when arrested. It was June 8, 1927.

Deciding further denials were useless, they confessed their identity and, while asserting their innocence waived extradition saying they wanted to go back to Oregon and clear their name. Their in-laws and friends were flabbergasted . . . those nice Goodwin boys from Arkansas were infamous murderers and train robbers from Oregon . . . the bloody DeAutremonts.

They didn't realize it at the time, but a one-time fellow worker had actually identified them and put the authorities on their trail. On Sunday, April 19, 1927, elderly Albert Collingsworth, who had only one eye and was in bed recuperating from the recent loss of both legs in a train accident, was reading the Portsmouth, Ohio *Times,* which contained a fascinating account of a 1923 train holdup in Oregon, resulting in the murder of four men. The crime had never been completely solved, although one of the three brothers suspected of the act had been recently captured in the Philippine Islands. It told of the world-wide search for the fugitives

Albert Collingsworth identified the Goodwin brothers as fugitives from Oregon.

Mrs. Emma L. Maynard, operator of the Maynard Detective Agency, in Ohio, who shared in the reward for the capture of Ray and Roy.

and showed pictures of the two men still wanted. On close examination of the pictures, to Mr. Collingsworth's astonishment, he recognized them as the Goodwin boys, with whom he had worked in the vicinity of Hanging Rock a year or so earlier. He called to his wife to come look at the pictures of the wanted men. She confirmed his identification.

A few days later, the knowledge was confided to his attorney, who advised Mr. Collingsworth to turn the information over to the authorities at once. In his crippled condition, he could get around only with the greatest difficulty, so he contacted Mrs. Emma L. Maynard, operator of the Maynard Detective Agency, and, after agreeing to split any reward fifty-fifty, the information was given to her. She immediately notified the Department of Justice in Columbus.

For some unknown reason there was considerable delay by the Department of Justice, but, eventually, they ascertained the brothers were then employed in Steubenville. The Steubenville police were approached for assistance and they went to the mill, where Roy walked into their hands.

Each of the six* men who helped arrest the twins received $100 of the reward money, with the $8,300 balance being divided between Mrs. Maynard and the crippled, but alert, Mr. Collingsworth. Even with only one eye, Mr. Collingsworth had been able to see better than thousands of others who had stared at the hundreds of thousands of posters plastered in barber shops, post offices, jewelry stores and employment offices throughout the country. The reward money he received was put to very good use and enabled him to purchase his artificial limbs.

Oddly enough, there had been several other reports, from the same vicinity, that one or other of the twins had been seen, but these had been too nebulous for follow-through.

Incidentally, the authorities moved about as slowly on the reward payment as they had on the capture, for the rewards were not paid until October, 1927, for all three boys. However, there were claims filed by 60 different individual, so perhaps there was good reason for the long delay, in sifting out just who deserved the reward.

*J.H. Bradstreet
Ross H. Cunningham
Wade Bougher
Ernest Schroeder
Thomas Bignam
Arthur Marshall

Chapter 11

Hugh's Flight and Capture

When 19-year-old Hugh whispered his quick goodbye to Roy at Grenada, California, and walked on down the road, he couldn't have helped but think of the complete fool he had been to let Ray talk him into such a stupid undertaking. However, at that point, regrets meant nothing and he could only make the best of the desperate situation.

Using the alias of James C. Price, which had been suggested by the name on a discarded baking powder can, hungry, shabby and weary, he continued south. He obtained a few days' work from a farmer, helping put up hay, which provided a little pocket money and enabled him to purchase some decent clothing. Eventually, he arrived at Long Beach, where he found a job with a construction company. Everywhere he went though, reward posters stared menacingly at him as a reminder of his terrible predicament, and people were still constantly discussing the attempted train robbery and the horrible murders which had occurred in the mountains of southern Oregon.

On New Year's Day, 1924, Hugh nervously called at the general delivery window of the Santa Ana Post Office, inquiring for any mail for James C. Price. After a few agonizing moments, he was advised there was none. He thought that possibly his brothers were dead and did not again try for contact at Santa Ana.

From Long Beach, the young fugitive drifted to Mexicali, giving some thought to escape into Mexico. Having failed to make contact with the twins as planned, he decided to go farther east, where the crime wouldn't be so much on people's minds. Hitching a ride on a freight train, he traveled to Arizona and then on into Texas, working a few days at a time, when and where work could be found. Eventually, he reached Emmett, Arkansas, the state of his birth some 20 years earlier. During the couple of weeks he worked at Emmett, he made the acquaintance of 17-year old William Adams, whose name would later play a minor role in his capture.

Leaving Arkansas, he "beat" his way through Missouri, on to the east coast and then, as the weather turned cold, south into Louisiana. Always the threat of capture was on his mind; he was afraid to stay anyplace more than a few days at a time and could trust no one, nor share his burden of guilt and fear.

During April 1924, he drifted to the north again. While on a freight train in Arkansas a policeman stopped him for questioning, but he pursuaded the officer he was in a hurry to visit a sick brother and was let go without further checking. He finally reached Chicago where he wandered the streets, cold and hungry, looking for a job. The mass of people seemed overwhelming and the city too threatening. It was not a town he liked. On one occasion, while strolling around looking for something to do, he inadvertently entered a particularly tough-looking neighborhood. To his consternation, a friendly policeman advised him it was no place for a nice young man like him and provided a safe escort from the area. The humor of the situation was not lost on Hugh, but he easily refrained from laughter.

During this wandering throughout Chicago, his eye was attracted by a recruiting poster for the U.S. Army, showing the balmy tropics, beautiful sandy beaches, with a background of waving palm trees. It appeared so inviting and seemed to offer a potential haven, where he could eat regularly and keep warm. Unquestionably, there would be great risks at the time of enlisting but he decided to chance it.

He gave his birthplace as Houston, Texas, and stated that he had no relatives; in case of an emergency, the Army was to notify William Adams, in Emmet, Arkansas. On April 22, 1924, he was sworn in and sent to nearby Ft. Sheridan, Illinois, where uniforms and equipment were issued. A few days later he shipped out to Ft. Slocum, New York, and then by boat to The Presidio, California, the point of embarkation for the Philippine Islands.

While at The Presidio, there were a couple of very narrow escapes, the first occurring when a Post Office Inspector came through the barracks talking to various soldiers, but passed by Hugh. The second instance was when another soldier laughingly called his attention to one of the DeAutremont reward posters on the base, commenting how much the one fellow resembled Private James C. Price.

The chance to eat regularly again and sleep in a warm, comfortable bed each night was a welcome change for the young recruit who had been desperately on the run for six months. The placid boat ride across the Pacific was an exciting surcease from worry. Viewing so much water was quite a thing for a youngster from the dry country of New Mexico, and the occasional flying fish darting across the ocean near the ship amazed and delighted him. After a quick stop in Honolulu, the ship arrived in Manila, P. I., where Hugh was assigned to Company B, 31st Infantry.

The young man was a good soldier, an excellent athlete, and quite popular with the men in his outfit, even though he was considered something of a braggart and teller of fanciful tales. While he had become more confident in his camouflaged life, he was always careful not to drink too much and constantly kept on the alert to keep from making a slip which might inadvertently betray him. One of his best friends was a likable youngster from Arkansas, named Jack Vick, who had fibbed about his age and joined the Army while only 15 years old. He would later play a somewhat poignantly tragic role in Hugh's life.

Late in June 1926, Sgt. Thomas Reynolds, lately of Company B, 31st Infantry, arrived in San Francisco, to await reassignment, prior to discharge. A few days later, on July 2nd, he was standing in front of the Company bulletin board, idly glancing at the items there when he was stunned to recognize a picture of Private James C. Price staring at him from a reward poster. Carefully, he read and re-read the description. It matched perfectly. Even the alias of E.E. James had an obvious relationship to James C. Price.

Taking the boat to San Francisco, he went to the Southern Pacific Building, where he talked to William H. Stone, declaring he knew the whereabouts of Hugh DeAutremont. Excited by what seemed to be a really worthwhile clue, Stone hurried Sgt. Reynolds to the nearby Postal Inspector's office, where the story was repeated with the Sergeant being very convincing about Hugh's long-concealed identity.

The Post Office Inspector's office immediately contacted the Army for further information on the suspected soldier, and the data were found to be extremely skimpy: he had enlisted in Chicago, on April 22, 1924, giving his birthplace as Houston, Texas, and in case of an emergency, William Adams, at Emmett, Arkansas, was to be notified. No record could be found of his birth in Houston. Checking on William Adams, the only such-named person they could locate was a former resident of Emmett who stated James C. Price was unknown to him.

Inasmuch as the identity of Price was neither proven nor disproven, on Nov. 17, 1926, the case was assigned to Inspector Fred Smith, with instructions to follow through by going to Manila to determine for certain if the suspected soldier actually was the long-elusive Hugh DeAutremont.

About this time Hugh received a letter from a former buddy, advising him the authorities were checking on him and if he was in some sort of trouble, to watch out. Hugh never revealed who the person was, although he took no action in response to the warning. Soon thereafter, he was called into the orderly room to have his picture taken and knew the long evasion was about to end. His discharge was due in just a few more months and he felt, if it were possible to avoid apprehension before then, he might get away to China and elude the authorities. However, time had run out for him.

Left: When Private James Price of Company B, 31st Infantry, was called to have his picture taken, he suspected that the long chase was nearing an end.

Right: Jack Vick, the young friend of Hugh, from army days in the Philippine Islands, died from an accident while on his way to visit Hugh in Oregon.

Early in February, Inspector Smith arrived in Manila and, after conferring with Army officials, took Hugh into custody on February 11, 1927. Hugh was sent back to the States on the U.S. Transport **Thomas.** *(Hugh's young friend Jack Vick was also on the same boat, returning for discharge at the request of his parents for having enlisted without their approval while under age.)* They arrived in San Francisco on March 17, 1927. Hugh was then formally arrested and confined to the U. S. Disciplinary Barracks on Alcatraz Island.

While his identity was admitted, he disclaimed any knowledge of the crime or the whereabouts of his two brothers. Feeling the presence of his mother might help persuade the young man to confess, the Post Office and Southern Pacific shared in the expense of bringing Mrs. Belle DeAutremont from New Mexico to visit Hugh at Alcatraz. Mrs. DeAutremont was assured that if she could get the young prisoner to confess, it would be much easier for him. This meeting between Hugh and his mother lasted for some four hours, but Hugh's buddies had warned him that his conversations would be heard by the authorities. Despite assurances to the contrary, Inspector Jefferson had bored a hole into the room so he could listen from the library room next door. Hugh cautioned his mother that they were being overheard, by writing her a note, then he chewed up the note and swallowed it.

No usable information was obtained from the meeting and several agents were rather caustic in their comments about Mrs. DeAutremont's assistance and activities during the visit. They stated she didn't seem too worried about the fate of her young son, as she went to various shows in San Francisco and seemed to con-

U. S. Postal Inspector Tennyson Jefferson was very involved in the search for and prosecution of the elusive criminals.

sider the trip to be solely for her pleasure.

Under direct orders from Major J.K. Homer, no one was permitted on the island during this period without a special pass and no unauthorized person was allowed to speak to Hugh. On March 25, 1927, after eight days of interrogation and questions regarding his activities and whereabouts preceding the date of the crime, as well as the period from October 11, 1923 until the date of his arrest, he was turned over to Jackson County (Oregon) Sheriff Ralph Jennings. He was returned under heavy guard to Jackson County to stand trial.

As the handsome young prisioner was locked in the Jacksonville jail, numerous romantically inclined young ladies crowded nearby, excitedly eyeing the famous Hugh DeAutremont. Some of them daringly called out "Hello, Hugh", to be thrilled with a smile and a wave in return.

While awaiting trial Hugh wrote letters to some of his school chums and received heartening replies:

Artesia, N. Mex.
Sat. 2:30

Dear Hugh,

I am glad to hear from you - no foolin'. Have wanted to write a number of times but authorities differed as to your whereabouts so just kept putting it off. The arrival of your letter almost created a sensation. The news spread rapidly; small groups gathered quietly to discuss the matter, and the writer was pointed out by small boys on the street as one who had received a communication from the long absent "Morning Glory". Such, my boy, is fame. On the strength of my advance notices now, think I'll.. be able to crash Hollywood.

About our mutual friends: - Ed Welch finishes a four year
course in Vet Medicine and Surgery, at Ames this year. In June I
understand he graduated cum laude (Guess that'll hold you a
while. I had to look it up but its worth it. Kid Yeager throwed a
year there last year but dropped it as equine anatomy holds no
thrills. Can you feature Welsh as a Vet? He plans to engage in
small animal practice — to minister to the disorders of pet canines
and petted felines.

Craig Baker and Naylor are in Cal. They left with the avowed
purpose of seeing you when you came in but didn't have any luck,
I hear. Craig has been having a hell of a time since his mother
died. Luther Caraway married and his wife kicked the bucket.
Guy Steve has become our most sophisticated man about town —
a drug store cowboy of the first water (soda water). The Bee
Hunter, according to one of my trusted agents, is making quite a
noise at Texas A and M. this year - he plays a cornet. Preacher
Davis fell down an elevator shaft and the sudden step killed him,
they say. The lady of your dreams is unmarried, quite as lovely as
of yor and is now engaged in educational work at Atoka. I mean to
say she's teaching school on the rare occasions that I have convers-
ed with her she invariably express a desire & hope to hear from
you - a letter would not be amiss, I think. She is in the hills for a
few days at present but I will see her shortly. Her friend Lois M. is
now a buxom Matron (how have the mighty fallen) Welsh's sister
is married. The lecture on sarcasm was unnecessary - I'm a sen-
timentalist myself. About those signals - the state athletic
association has had men working on that secretly for the last four
years. If it is discovered that our opponents really did know
something about them we're going to challenge that last game of
1922. Rah Rah

The hinterlanders no longer conmingle at the Smoke House (oh
blessed memory) but gather nightly at the Sweet Shop - an institution where liquid refreshment of a percentage made obsolete
by Mr. Volstead, may be obtained by the knowing. (Thank God
for Prohibition. Well, Morning Glory for the sake of our own dear
Christ and my unbroken record of veracity, write me something of
your heroic action of the past year or so. In your travels did you
ever run across the Virgin Mary? If so, was she a blonde or
brunette. I want to get straightened out on that point. Even E.
Haldeman Julius won't say for sure.

That'll be all for this time. Let me know how it goes and I hope
thing break right on May 2. Adios

Yours until they make ethyl instead of methyl
Chig Yeager

Welch's address is
c/o Vet. Division
Iowa State College
Ames, Iowa.

Hugh's teen-age ambition had been to be an attorney and he was
now to have the opportunity to assist in practicing law with more
importance attached to the outcome than any other thing he would
ever again do, for his very life hung in the balance.

Trial for the first of the three accused brothers was set for May 2,
1927, with Circuit Court Judge C.M. Thomas presiding. Acting on

behalf of the prosecution was Newton C. Chaney, District Attorney; George Roberts, Assistant to the District Attorney and George Neuner, U.S. Attorney for the District of Oregon.

To defend the accused young man there were the following attorneys: Fred Smith, from Eugene, John Collier, of Portland, Gus Newbury, from nearby Medford and Dave Evans, of Eugene.

Newspaper reporters and curiosity seekers from all over gathered in the tiny town of Jacksonville, to watch the drama of the trial and the outcome of the last great train holdup in the West. Considerable sympathy was evident for the young accused.

Hugh's father was convinced of his son's innocence and endeavored to inspire the young prisoner:

4/19/1927

Paul DeAutremont
395 West 20th Avenue
Eugene, Oregon

Dear Hugh   Just a few lines, I am woking all the time & dont get much chance to write & then I am not giveing out aney information but we have won our first point so just sit pritty & we will have you out of there after this trial is over I dont expect them to bother you after this is over I know time is heavy over your head but this will come to an end some day and remember this & keep it in mind allways dainger only comes to test you it steels the nerves and test the man to conquest & to conquer, so go to your trial with that in mind & welcome the oppertunety to prove your innocence and that there is not one drop of craven blood in your veins & I will be with you when you meet the enemy face to face & we will not falter or flinch untill the victory is ours You have seene me time and time again win out when they give me no chance but courage nerve & fair fight & with Gods help we will win once again.
Never no Never say quit fight to the last & with our face to the foe & we will win

Dad

The following cryptic letter was received from a former sweetheart:

Los Angeles, California,
March 31st, 1927.

Hugh Dear,

I am trying to locate your mother.
Will you please tell her to write me or phone me at Beacon 8126 and charge it to me.
I want her address so please answer soon if you can. If you can't please have her get in touch with me.
I am home after five in the evening or before seven thirty in the

morning. It would be best if she dropped me a card or you can.
I want her address so I can write her.
Lots of love and best wishes.

Always your
Clara

Clara Pinkston
3036 3/4 Swift St.,
L. A.

This resulted in a further exchange of rather revealing letters:

Los Angeles, Calif.
April 21st, 1927

Hugh my love,

When I got home tonite and saw your letter lying here, I didn't
hurry much to read it. I usually read my mail before I get my hat
& coat off but I have been disappointed for more than two weeks
now on account of not hearing from mama. So I fooled around for
some time. Anyway I thot your letter would be postmarked San
Francisco. But what I am trying to tell you lover of long ago I was
tickled to death to get your letter.

But you didn't say where your mother was. I don't suppose you
tho't much of my letter but I had an awful time finding where and
how I could write you so finally I was told I could write you but I
couldn't say any thing much. Well I didn't did I but I am now.
You didn't tell me how to address the envelope so I want to be sure
you get this.

And I recognized your handwriting. You see I kept your other
letters until about 3 years ago then I destroyed them. Now I am
sorry.

When I read of your plight as I was walking down the streets of
El Paso one day I fainted on the walk and got my back wet as it
had been raining so you see I will have to get even with you by
writing you two letters instead of one.

And I wish you had of sent the other letters you destroyed.

And dear boy no thanks are coming for remembering you for I
have never forgotten you. I have been many many places and gone
with, met and seen many many boys and men but not a one has
taken your place in my heart and I wish to God I could come to
you this minute I would marry you (as ever thing stands now) if
you would ask me. I have never forgotten what you whispered one
nite so long ago when I said "In three years I will be 18," and you
said "and I will be 21" Can you wait that long. Oh Hugh the
sweetest words I ever heard were those. You know how I am how I
have always been. All smiles lots of giggles but underneath sen-
timental and sad. And I have had lots of experience and lots of
heart aches since I last saw you but do you know I seem to have
fattened & thrived on it all. I am still short, but a little heavier. I
have been working hard and helping support the chaildren and so
on but I love it all.

Not lets see. First dont think dear heart I am complaining about
a thing for I am not. I am just telling you so you will know the girl
that writing you. We lived on the Cottonwood when I saw you last,
from there to Dexter, then to Roswell from Roswell to El Paso
where we have been since. Papa tried farming and so on but it
went blooey. So I started working when I was seventeen and have

been ever since. But I got tired of the old hot tin can and wanted to come to L. A. So I finally got away from Mama and started to seek my fortune. I have been here a year and a half. Now my oldest sister Orlean & my little brother (he was little when you knew him) are here with me. I lived alone for a long time. I think the folks will be all be here next month but they will live in Long Beach. I am working and have been ever since I have been here at the R. L. Polk and Co. of Calif. a Direct Mail place

I have lots to tell you when I see you and I know I shall some day if you want me to. I am disappointed however for I tho't I should see you soon at Frisco.

Well I'll try to find a picture for you but I am afraid you will be a bit disappointed. But I will take a chance And don't think I havent one of your pictures. I have.

Now I will try and answer your questions. The first I have answered partly I am in charge of the mailing department but I dont think I will be very long for I dont like it. So a change as soon as possible.

2-I have been in L. A. 1½ yrs.

3 No I am not married. I was engaged to a sweet boy once but he died in February of pneumonia three years ago. But I did not love him.

4- And the simple reason was. I never could quiet banish you from my heart. You were my first and you shall be my last.

5-And my dear you shall see me again. Some day, I know, **now if** I had the money. And I shall consult the crystal gazer as soon as I can get to her. ha ha

6- I never heard a word from the young man after he left there. I would not kiss him goodby after him riding from Lakewood to Artesia. So I suppose he was peeved but you know I felt then it was wrong to kiss one you did not love. I hated lies and it have seemed so much a lie if I had. I had to laugh at the remembrance of how you and I laughted when you told me what he said.

7- I have told you about all I could. You know I could write on and on but I had rather wait and tell you.

8- Do I still love you. Hugh you know I do and you know I will always. I used to tell my Mother when I was so young that she laughed at me that my heart was all yours if I never did get to see you again. Of course she laughed but she admitted many times she would always have a soft spot in her heart for you.

9 No answer to this question.

10 But plenty to this.

11- Yes we were as loveable as kids could be but I tho't we were quite grown up. Do you remember when you first talked to me and took me to supper and wanted me to sit down on a board to eat and I wouldn't do it. I told you I didn't want to soil my dress. Well now I will tell you the truth. I stole my mother's long old corset and wore it to the dance and I couldn't stoop low enough down to sit. Gosh but I was embarrased and thrilled also. I was so afraid I wouldn't please you. I tho't I was quiet grown up and, etc. Remember the carnival we went to at Carlsbad and listen do you remember one night when we were out side on my folding bed and you stuck your tie pin in the edge of the bed. Well I kept that pin until I wore the pin off of it then when it broke I was going to have a ring made and put the stone in but in moving once I left it in a tiny purse and never went back to the place any more. I suppose

the people still have it. But we had a fuss and I wouldn't go back
12- Yes I will send photo.
13 Were you not at all surprised to hear from me. No dear we can
not look for surprises any more for they would be many. So just
take things as they come and Hugh don't forget God for he knows
and understands. I am not religious I never go to church and Sunday School because I think I should but I don't forget there is a
God in Heaven. And I can swear also. So you see what I mean dont
you.
14- Yes often I have dreamed of when we were together. I used to
live for my dreams for it seemed when we were parted part of my
life had been taken and often I would ask God if you had forgotten.

Well now Hugh if I would tell you I was pretty you would say I
was conseited. I have been and am now always being told I am
pretty but you know flattery never turned my head. If I am I am
glad. If not I am glad also. Of course dear boy we like for some people to say nice things. I do have a good reputation however of having beautiful legs. Now don't blush for I am not conceited about
that either. I know you are just as handsome and sweet as always.

Now Hugh I know a lot of peoples affairs and troubles and am
broad minded as ever thing so what I am going to say don't take it
wrong. Please for if you do it will break my heart. I want to know
as frankly as I ask. Have you any money and do you need some.
You know that I can't do much for you except write you and send
you money or things to read and so on so please don't deny me this
if you need it.

You write me a lovely letter and I will keep it and cherish it and
I want you to write me soon as you can and answer my questions
and ask as many as you like for sweetheart I havent a thing to do
but answer. And I shall.

Hugh I don't know how to end this there is so much to be said
that can't be and so many years have gone by and and oh well
whats the use. Lover mine be as cheerful as you can and don't take
my letter wrong. Take it just as it is meant will you promise just
this. I will be expecting an answer real soon. So until I do please
don't forget your old sweetheart who ever cares and who understands always. Your sweet chicken.
                          Clara

Remember when you called me sweet chicken also the prunes and
hair pins and say I haven't even seen my chum Ola Mae since the
night you kissed me so hard on sore lips at her house. Remember I
will be happy and waiting for your reply. do it too.
                          Clara

How far are you from me and will you be there for some time and
how are your folks at home.
      Tell me all you can please
                          C

Hugh quickly replied:

                                                  Same Place
                                                  April 26, 27.
Dear Little Girl
      I will frankly say that I am broke, having made an affadavit to
that effect. Will also add that I don't need any coin of the realm.

And I surely thank you for your kind offer. Bless your heart. Dam this pen.

My trial opens May 2nd. It may take several days to complete the jury. As to the actual time needed to close the case- I can't say but don't think it will be much before the latter part of the month. Now, dear heart, as to how long I'll be here- draw your own conclusion.

As to my location, sweetheart, consult a map. I am five miles west of Medford, Oregon.

And darling I do think of God. I am always saying God- this and God that & etc. But I shall not lift my hands to that invested bowl we call the sky, for help as it as impotently moves as you or I. He understands and all well.

I need love, sympathy and a shave and if your money could furnish any of the above I'd say "Slip me". But I have a hunch you can use all you earn. And where did you get that old fashioned idea of opologizing for offering aid? Oh, bless your heart.

We had a wedding here the other day. The bridegroom was & is an inmate of this institution. A very touching scene. How ever must say- Its a dam poor place for a honey moon. Otherwise dear girl I'd surely take you up on your pleasant suggestion And Sweetheart I do appreciate the spirit which prompted you to throw yourself on the altar of sacrifice. But in fairness to you, sweet child I must, sadly tis true, let that idea go by the board, as it were. You must, I'm sure, understand- and were circumstances different I thing your maiden life would come to a very abrupt halt. I knew that I'd made some impression on your heart but did not know how lasting it was until I rec'd your letter. However it is mutual, dear one, as I have never forgotten our happy days on the Rio Pecos.

Hope springs eternal in the human breast- So let us hope. Who knows, but some day all your dreams'll come true. If not shall we suffer more for having hoped? I suppose so.

The picture of you (on the wagon) looks as I remember you- very pretty indeed- also noticed the liberal view of those ah-er- pedal extremities of which you spoke. They are lovely and all you claimed for them- allow me to add my compliments. The one (with two boy friends) is not so good. You look sad, somewhat, methinks- and a trifle-er plump. No fooling, how much do you weigh. Besides your means of locomotion were not included here. They were both good the pictures I mean, however. Thanx

You have not bobbed your hair or the picture is a liar. God be praised. Or have you bobbed it in the past & now letting it grow? Anyway let me say that you are very much O. K. even if flattery don't turn your pretty head.

I heard about a girl fainting in El Paso, upon hearing of my plight and I was sure it was u. I did not faint but let me assure you that I certainly experienced some thrilling & unique sensations. Don't we have fun?

I just re-read your letter and if I read between the lines correctly let me say. Use your own judgement.

So the boy you were engaged to died? Can you give me the fates of some of your other admirers?

Yes I remember all the incidents you mentioned & if I may be so bold- well a few more.

Who was the wise guy who said that to part with one you loved was dying a little? Of course he was right, don't you think?

Dearest if you think I am as handsome as per yore- well brace
yourself- I am not. If that didn't floor you for the count, duck- And
I am not the lad you knew in N. M. for I am not what you described as sweet. However in your cheerful company methinks I could
recover bye and bye. And by the way do you remember the beating
I rec'd in the squared ring at Carlsbad?

I am glad you care & understand. Only of course you don't and
can't understand but I love you for thinking you do. And of course
I'll take your letter the way you intend for me to. But I won't try to
be cheerful if I feel otherwise. I am going to be myself. More power
to me. At the present I'll say the writer is far from being despondent. Tis raining and the gods are crying for us, Clara, let them do
the weeping. I'd cry too if I'd ever treated any one as they treat us.
They should be ashamed. Perhaps their remorse shall make them
straighten our tangled fates- or quite obliterate- I must not
become poetic. May our sun never set
Hugh

P. S.
I'd like to, you loveable imp- But why torture me. And don't pre-
tend to misunderstand
Love H

P. P. S. April 27
I just left Mother- She wrote you some time ago. A letter sent to
Medford will reach her. I am about 400 miles from Frisco. The sun
is shining this morning & all is O. K. By the way dont you think
that if you was to tell his honor what a good guy I was and am and
incidently give him a liveral view of those beautiful limbs clad in
sheer silk hoisery & et- you know- he would dismiss the case-eh.

Hurray for our side.

Being broad minded you won't take offence to anything I say
but will remember I love you
H.

Ironically, the widespread publicity from Hugh's capture
triggered the capture of the twins in Ohio a few weeks later. For the
first time since that miserable morning along the Klamath River, in
November 1923 when cold, hungry, ragged, dirty, tired and
desperate, the three brothers had reluctantly shaken hands and
said goodbye, they were to meet again in the Jacksonville jail. It
was another of the many strange quirks of fate in this crime.

The boys, while separated half way around the world, were captured with such timing that all learned their fate almost at the
same moment - just as they had committed their crime - together.

There was another strange coincidence revolving around the year
1927 and its fateful relationship to the DeAutremont family. On
March 1, 1927, Lee DeAutremont, the youngest of the 5 boys, was
accidentally killed in San Angelo, Texas, by a man named Stewart,
during a shooting brawl in an oilfield gambling house. C. E.
Thompson, Orient Railway Special Agent, was keeping the
youngest DeAutremont under surveillance at the time, in case he
had any contact with the wanted brothers. Mrs. Belle DeAutremont
came from Arcadia, N. M., to take charge of the body and burial.

Chapter 12

Hugh's First Trial

Initially, Hugh related a rambling story of the three boys having been operating an illegal "moonshine still" on the mountain and fleeing when a posse approached their operation. Learning then of the train holdup and murders, it was decided to leave the area until enough money could be obtained for a proper defense, as they were afraid of being suspected of the crime. Whichever of the three first earned enough money was to return and clear up the case.

Such an unlikely story was quickly discredited through Hugh's contradictory statements but he still denied participation in the crime. The nearest thing to any admission of guilt was an inadvertent outburst to his mother, overheard while at Alcatraz, following her urging him to "make a clean breast" of everything, when he replied, "No, no, Mother, don't let them talk you into that," and then, later, "Mother, you didn't ever think your 19-year-old boy would go wrong, but I didn't mean to do it."

By 7:30 a.m. on the morning of Monday, May 2, 1927, curiosity seekers were lined up outside the stately old Jackson County Court House, in the tiny, gold-rush town of Jacksonville, to watch the proceedings. The high-ceilinged courtroom was jammed to capacity, with 150 spectators crowded into the old-fashioned, raw-hide bottomed chairs placed in neat rows across the room. The County Clerk's chair offered considerable contrast, the seat containing a homemade, be-ruffled cushion, feather-stitched in bright yellow and, obviously, providing considerably more posterial comfort than others in the room.

The press section was somewhat less than "swanky", but then the little town was not accustomed to such needs. It consisted of long boards, placed lengthwise across a pair of saw-horses, at one side of the room. On the opening day, a dozen or so full bottles of ink were thoughtfully placed along the table, despite the fact that most reporters, in those days, used soft lead pencils for taking notes. On the second day, the ink bottles had quietly vanished.

Brightly polished brass cuspidors were placed conveniently at the front of the jury box, with others strategically scattered around near

Left: Circuit Court Judge C. M. Thomas presided at Hugh's trial and sentenced the three brothers.

Right: Attorney George M. Roberts spearheaded the prosecution at Hugh's trial.

the Judge and attorneys, so there could be no excuse for wayward streams of tobacco juice.

At 9:30 a.m., the big doors at the south corner of the Court House opened and the neatly dressed, smiling, debonair young defendant entered, his military training obvious as he marched erectly across the room to the defense table. He was followed by Ralph Jennings, the Jackson County Sheriff.

In the audience, near the court railing, sat Mrs. DeAutremont, conservatively dressed in a tan jersey dress, a brown bolivia coat and a tan and green hat. While she was much darker than her son, there was a considerable resemblance. Uncertainly, she arose and moved over to sit quietly beside her son.

Hugh carefully watched as the attorneys began examinations of the prospective jurors, which continued through the morning with only a ten minute recess. Occasionally, Hugh would lean over and whisper a question to one of his attorneys. The court recessed at noon, with news cameramen lining up the respective groups for the defense and prosecution for picture-taking. Theatre patrons across the country had a vicarious look-see at the dramatic proceedings, just after the cartoons and preceding the feature movie.

The good ladies of the Eastern Star Lodge participated in the event by serving a hot box lunch at their nearby headquarters. Mrs. DeAutremont ordered a meal for her son, and Ike Dunford, the jailer, thoughtfully carried it back to the jail cell on a tray. Spring is a particularly beautiful time in the Rogue Valley and the flowers at the nearby homes were in colorful bloom. Many spectators brought their own lunches, gathered on the green lawn surrounding the Court House, and, beneath the lovely shade trees, ate and discussed the exciting situation at hand. It was the most dramatic event in the area since the trial of the Ku Klux Klan members, and even that didn't hold a candle by comparison.

Each prospective juror was carefully questioned by the opposing attorneys. There was a great reluctance on the part of many potential jurors to convict on circumstantial evidence alone, and it was obvious the prosecution would be basing much of its case on the scientific research of Professor Heinrich. The prosecution used five of its six peremptories and the defense used ten of its twelve peremptories but, after three days of courtroom maneuvering, and the examination of more than 200 prospective jurors, 12 men were finally selected:

> Albert Piche, Medford merchant
> S. E. Heberling, Central Point
> E. N. Judy, Griffin Creek retired farmer
> Nick W. Kime, Medford farmer
> B. M. Bush, Willow Springs electrician
> S. W. Dunham, Medford clerk
> C. W. Davis, City of Medford Employee
> A. W. Ward, Eagle Point farmer
> Frank Earhart, Medford farmer
> James E. Clemens, Medford orchardist
> Fred Fredenburg, Medford teamster
> F. W. Wiley, Central Point merchant.

The jurors were assigned to a suite of rooms at the Hotel Holland, in Medford, where they were to remain until dismissed by the Court. They were to be deprived of all newspapers and communications, except through the court bailiffs. They were instructed not to discuss the case, even among themselves.

Paul DeAutremont arrived Wednesday morning to see his son for the first time since October 1923, and was eagerly awaiting Hugh's entry into the courtroom, whereupon he dramatically rushed forward to embrace his boy, much to the young man's embarrassment. During the day the father sat next to his son, with his arm around the young defendent's shoulders. As Paul sat down, he leaned across and shook hands with his former wife, long-time animosities pushed aside in a common cause.

On Thursday, May 5th, the trial actually began, with the State bringing forth item after item of evidence. Nominally, the charge was the murder of Charles Oran Johnson (the slain brakeman), but it was necessary to prove the defendant had actually been at the crime scene and had participated in its execution. Numerous ladies of the audience were properly nauseated when Dr. Holt, the former Jackson County Coroner, who was employed by the prosecution in the investigation of the crime, testified how, at the request of Newton C. Chaney, District Attorney, the body of Johnson, buried for almost four years, had been dug up two weeks previously; how he had reexamined it at the edge of the grave; how the slugs were taken from the body, to be used as evidence.

Following a long elaboration on the wounds throughout the body, the angle of the bullets, etc., Dr. Holt claimed unfamiliarity with firearms and ammunition and couldn't classify the missiles found in the body. One elderly juror, displaying impatience with the boring, lengthy, discussions as to the type of missiles, finally leaned forward and snapped, "Well, was it buckshot you found or what?" The doctor, smiling, replied, "I couldn't say as to that."

Frank Ramirez, Southern Pacific Investigator, took the stand and testified to having arrived on the scene of the crime the day following and, with his men, having made an exhaustive search of the surrounding vicinity in an effort to locate every possible clue.

Among the items of evidence he identified were fired cartridge cases, picked up at the tunnel and at the two camps where the suspects were supposed to have stayed prior to the crime. In addition, there were cooking utensils, iron straps and hinges from the burned chest supposedly belonging to Hugh, creosote-soaked footpads, knapsacks and a DuPont detonater. The black grip found in the nearby underbrush, on the bottom of which was posted a Wells Fargo sticker, and a drab-colored cap, a spool of black thread, and so forth, were each, in turn, introduced, examined and placed into evidence.

Attorney John Collier carefully quizzed Ramirez and, when a pair of blue bib-overalls were Introduced and identified by the investigator, Collier really went to work on him, as this was one of the State's key items. Ramirez admitted he had not thoroughly examined the overalls. However, he stated they had been in his possession and, according to Dan O'Connell's instructions, he had taken them to Professor Heinrich for examination, along with the foot pads, automatic pistol and knapsacks. *(On October 26, 1923, in an interview with a reporter from the Eugene Guard, Dan O'Connell stated there was no foundation to the report of a postal money order receipt having been found in the discarded clothing left at the scene of the attempted holdup. This incongruity was never explained but it is assumed Mr. O'Connell was endeavoring to conceal the fact that a tremendously vital bit of evidence had been discovered.)*

Vincent Arcega, also an investigator for the Southern Pacific, testified to having reached the site of the crime on October 12th, and, in the company of Charles Moore, of the Oregon National Guard, and Victor Dale, to having carefully searched the adjacent

areas. He identified the creosote-stained pan, found at the Mt.
Crest cabin, along with the black grip, cap, Colt pistol and cartridges.

A multitude of items were introduced, including old tin cups,
knives, forks, spoons, rusty skillets and rusty frying pans, together
with an empty Mazola Oil can, which wracked the audience with
laughter when the bombastic George Neuner exposed his lack of
knowledge, as, holding up the Mazola can, he emphatically
proclaimed, "Everybody knows Mazola is used for oiling guns."

Attorney Fred Smith leaned over to his colleague and in a stage
whisper facetiously commented, "Neuner sees himself in the Governor's chair," - a pointed reference to the voluminous state-wide
publicity connected with the case and Neuner's little-concealed
political ambitions.

There were several references by the prosecution to a rind of
bacon found in a pan at the Mt. Crest cabin, which caused Hugh to
remark wryly, "They've brought in everything but the bacon."

During the long and frequently dull sessions of presenting and
labeling minute items of questionable importance, the men on the
jury struggled to keep their interest from flagging. Some of them insisted on personally examining the evidence. There was one man,
solidly bent on comfort, who kept his shoes off, periodically wriggl-
ing his toes as if to keep them from going to sleep, as he was wont to
do; another methodically munched peanuts from a large sack at his
feet . . . he didn't even share with his peers on the jury, but perhaps
the working of his jaws kept his brain also in operation; and then
there was the marvelous description, by a newspaper writer covering the trial, of

" . . . the man who chewed gum from nine until five. He
chewed through the display of kitchen utensils. He chewed through each of the sixty-three bullets, the wire, the
hinges, the iron rods. He chewed through the black grip
with its needle and spool of black thread; through the
brown cap and blue overalls. He smiled and chewed, and
frowned and chewed, he shifted and chewed, and dozed
and chewed. He chewed through the battles, between the
battles of the counsels, and rulings of the judge."

At that point, even the reporters needed spirited imaginations to
create a degree of interest.

The attorneys frequently clashed in heated exchanges. Collier
repeatedly raised objections to evidence introduced by Neuner.
Once, after a series of objections by Collier, Neuner thoroughly irk-
ed Collier by condescendingly smiling and commenting, "Now,
John, all I'm trying to do is introduce evidence."

A dramatic confrontation took place when Collier cross-examined
L. D. Forncrook, deputy sheriff at the time of the crime, regarding
the overalls found at the robbery scene. Collier picked up the

overalls, stuck his finger into the bib pocket and held them up before the witness, as prosecutor Roberts had done, and asked, "Did you need anyone to call your attention to this pocket?"

Attorneys Roberts and Neuner jumped to their feet quickly objecting, but Judge Thomas overruled them. Collier repeated the question.

"No."

"Did you examine this pocket at the time?"

"Yes."

"And, you found nothing in it?"

"No."

"That's all," said Collier, tossing the overalls to the floor in a contemptuous, grandstand gesture at the believability of the evidence offered, for the bib pocket was the one which the prosecution claimed had held the registered mail receipt initially linking the DeAutremonts to the murders and attempted robbery.

One sadly poignant witness was Mrs. Blanche Rinabarger (former wife of E. E. Dougherty, the slain mail clerk) who wept on the stand as she identified pictures of her dead husband.

Jack Vick, Hugh's under-age Army buddy, arrived in Jacksonville, eager to testify on behalf of the good character of his friend. The youngster had hitch-hiked from Sacramento to Jacksonville, arriving penniless and quite shabby. Miss Mary Greiner, a vivacious, young newspaper reporter covering the trial, felt sorry for Vick's lack of proper clothing and persuaded some of her friends to outfit him with something more presentable for his courtroom appearance.

On Friday, the courtroom was crowded beyond capacity with people fascinated by the drama of the slight youth confronting the combined forces of the Southern Pacific and U. S. Post Office Department, but Judge Thomas, with a Solomon-like ruling, quickly solved the problem of overcrowding by ordering all high school students expelled from the room and commanding them to return to their classes. The students retaliated on Saturday by returning at an early hour to make sure of seats, and it was necessary to install extra chairs in front of the Press table to take care of the overflow audience.

Many of those in the audience were obviously quite sympathetic to the young, good-looking defendant and, each time the big, burly, blue-jowled Southern Pacific investigators were on the stand, the crowd showed itself partisan in his behalf. From a safe distance, young flappers outrageously flirted with him, but this soon became such a common occurrence that, in most instances, he merely gave them a quiet smile. At that moment, there were things on his mind far more important than young ladies, no matter how pretty or friendly they might be.

On the night of Friday, May 6, 63-year-old jury member, S. W. Dunham, fell ill. Following treatment by a physician, he returned to the jury box on Saturday morning, but obviously he was still not well, and the 12 noon adjournment gave considerable relief to him, as well as the court. It was hoped he would be totally recovered by the time court reconvened on Monday.

The ailing juror did return on Monday but, as the trial proceeded, he became weaker and weaker and, again by noon, it was necessary for two other jurors to support him on his way from the courtroom. That afternoon, Judge Thomas called for a recess and ordered him taken home, where he could be treated by his physician until totally recovered.

On Wednesday, May 11, Dunham died at his home and, that same day, Judge Thomas declared a mistrial and set June 25 for a continuance.

Chapter 13

The Second Trial

On May 25, Judge Thomas announced that the date for Hugh's new trial had been set ahead to June 6. This surprise change of date was very disconcerting to the defense attorneys, who claimed witnesses would not be available that quickly, as they had scattered; many people would be on vacation and the trial should be postponed until September, but the Judge ruled against such pleas and the new trial proceeded as ordered.

The attorneys were able to select 12 jurors without going through such a lengthy and traumatic session as of the first trial, and by 3:30 p.m., on June 6, the 12 men chosen were empaneled, although they were not sworn in until 9:00 a.m., the following day. None of the original jury members were on the second jury:

Henry W. Frame, Phoenix	R.A. Wideman, Eagle Point
W.W. Hittle, Gold Hill	R.S. Daniels, Medford
Fred B. Dutton, Medford	L.O. Norcross, Ashland
William F. Darby, Ashland	Paul W. Marin, Central Point
Earl W. Weaver, Central Point	Frank Miller, Ashland
Thomas Farlow, Lake Creek	M.J. Kerney, Central Point

It was, of course, necessary for the prosecution to begin the entire case over again and, as court opened on June 10, prosecutor George Roberts launched the session with an hour and a half opening statement. Slowly, deliberately and with agonizingly infinite detail, he led the jury through a complete review of the crime, from the most gruesome details of the killings and the condition of the bodies, to the May mistrial caused by the unfortunate death of Mr. Dunham.

Chief defense counsel Fred Smith made many points with the audience, and probably the jury, by replying to the long opening statement by the prosecution with a very brief five-minute opening statement, addressing the jury and concluding with, "We challenge the State to bring in any evidence bearing upon the crime that has any connection whatsoever with the defendant here before you." He then sat down. Circumstantial evidence was not as generally accepted by most people in 1927 as it has since become, and one of the major needs of the prosecution was to convince the jury absolutely of Hugh's presence at the crime, as well as of his actual participation in its execution.

Paul DeAutremont arrived at the Court House with Hugh's eleven-year-old step-sister and five-year-old half-brother Charles, children of his second wife. Both of them adored Hugh and enthusiastically hugged him as he laughingly kidded and joked with them.

Jack Vick, Hugh's teen-age army friend, spent the period between trials working in Eugene but returned to the courtroom, where he sat quietly in the audience. In his recently acquired brown suit, he was ready and anxious to provide any help possible for Hugh.

The State's first witness was Herbert M. Micander, Southern Pacific Engineer, of Dunsmuir, who had been dead-heading on the ill-fated train # 13 at the time of the hold up, and who described the discovery of the bodies scattered around the exit of the tunnel. He was followed by George C. Stevens, conductor; James Benjamin, the rear brakeman, who had found Roy's dropped pistol at the tunnel's east entrance; Samuel L. Clayton, conductor; Hugh Haffey, expressman and John W. Mitchell, trainman. Even H. B. Carter, who had been cleaning fish in the train kitchen at the moment of the holdup, was called to testify.

On June 8, a report was received that Roy and Ray had been apprehended in Ohio and were, at that moment, on their way back to Jacksonville. *(There is some conflict on the exact date the twins were arrested, with some sources stating June 7 and some June 8. Southern Pacific records state the arrest took place on June 8.)*

As they were unable to post the $50,000 bail, on June 9, 1927, Deputy U.S. Commissioner C. J. Barrow ordered the twins taken from the Steubenville jail to the Franklin County jail in Columbus, to await the arrival of the Oregon authorities. However, it was later decided the Steubenville jail was secure enough and the prisoners were not moved until June 17, when they left in the custody of Sheriff Ralph Jennings, his Chief Deputy Louis Jennings (his son) and four other officers.

When questioned as to his thoughts on the arrest report, Hugh replied, "Honestly, I've heard so much and the papers say so much . . . I have come to this . . . that you can't believe anything." In a subsequent interview with Mrs. Belle DeAutremont about the reported capture of the twins, she stated, "I can't express to you how I feel. But perhaps you'll understand. I have been so firmly convinced, for such a long, long time that my boys were dead . . . especially Roy . . . that it will take more proof than this to make me believe them alive." She smiled then, and added excitedly, "But, if they are alive, they can't get here soon enough to suit me."

A steady stream of witnesses for the State marched to the stand, many with infinitesimal scraps of unimportant information, others of highly questionable authenticity. There was D. J. Parker, the picturesque, 70-year-old placer miner from Siskiyou County (California), who blithely claimed that the night following the train holdup, he had been stopped by Hugh at his claim on Elliott Creek (some 30 miles from the holdup site), and, at the point of a gun, robbed of his gold cleanup. While he was a colorful character, his testimony was not overly convincing and, the following day, another miner from the same area, Ed Foster, testified that not only was Parker's eyesight poor, but he had originally described the thief to Foster as being bearded, muscular and six feet tall. There were also the two witnesses claiming to have seen Hugh in the vicinity of the tunnel, the night prior to the crime, but their validity was considered quite questionable.

Dr. E. O. Heinrich, with his scientifically oriented testimony, contributed heavily to the mass of evidence and weighed greatly against the young defendant.

John McCracken, a mechanic during September 1923, at the Park Garage in Ashland, provided some telling testimony in stating that Hugh, calling himself E. E. James, brought a damaged Nash automobile into the garage on September 26, 1923, declaring he had struck a cow and needed the car repaired as quickly as possible. He described Hugh and the clothing worn at the time.

A string of witnesses continued, with various railroad employees, people connected with sales to the boys of numerous items which had been brought in as evidence, and on and on.

H. H. McCullogh and H. C. Grat, employees of the Silver Falls Lumber Company, in Silverton, testified to knowing Hugh and his brothers and to their having left together. A. E. Gerinmonte, time keeper and bookkeeper for the lumber company, identified Hugh as E. E. James, who had worked there during the summer of 1923, and testified that the three had left on the same day in August.

Seventy-year-old O. H. Hitchcock, who made the bunkhouse beds at the lumber company, told of noticing the strangely shaped iron straps on the odd-looking, wooden chest of Hugh's; of having been in a room next to the one occupied by the three brothers and of peeking through a crack to see Hugh (alias E. E. James) cleaning a pistol; and that the trunk contained boxes of cartridges. He claimed to have later slipped into the room where a copy of *The Life of Jesse James* was found on the table, which he proceded to read. Straps of iron, found near the Mt. Crest cabin, where things had been burned, were identified by him as having been those seen on Hugh's chest.

Charlie Terrill, Jackson County Sheriff at the time of the crime, was called to the stand, as well as were many other law enforcement officials and local residents.

Ray and Roy, with Jackson County Sheriff Ralph Jennings, posing in front of the County Jail, in Jacksonville.

The courtroom tenseness was broken on the 17th, when the springs on Judge Thomas's chair snapped with a loud bang, thoroughly startling everyone and evoking a great burst of laughter at the Judge's expense.

There was testimony regarding the registered mail receipt for the letter sent by Roy to his brother Verne in Lakewood, enclosing a life insurance policy. R. H. Craddock, a Portland firearms expert, testified that the slugs taken from trees at Silverton and on the Siskiyous had been compared and were fired from the same weapon.

Efforts on behalf of the defense were painfully weak. There was a parade of character witnesses and Mrs. L. J. Morton, an elderly rooming house operator, stated she believed the three boys had been at her house in Eugene from September 26th to October 10th, some 234 miles (at that time) distant from the location of the crime. However, her records showed evidence of erasures and she confessed to being a poor record keeper.

Mary K. Sands, a teacher at the Montana State Normal School, and a former High School teacher of Hugh's, came to testify for him as a character witness.

Around mid-morning on June 21, the twins arrived at the Jacksonville jail, in company with Post Office Inspectors George Pate, S. R. Kelchner and A. W. Deming, together with Sheriff Ralph Jennings. Enroute from Ohio, the personable twins became quite friendly with their escorts and discussed the thought of pleading guilty to a charge of first degree murder and accepting a

The Jackson County Courthouse as it appeared in 1927, at the time of Hugh's trial.

sentence of life imprisonment, should the trial of Hugh result in his conviction with a like sentence. Later, Roy stated that the escort had treated them so thoughtfully that any idea of escaping was discarded, although there had been opportunities to do so.

While Hugh was inside the courthouse with his attorneys making their final desperate efforts on his behalf, unbeknown to him the twins were being lodged in the jail next door, only a few yards away. Within a few minutes after the cell doors closed on them, they were enthusiastically singing a duet, "Father Don't Have to Work In The Mines Today."

Reporters quickly obtained permission to interview the newly-arrived prisoners and, upon meeting the smiling pair, were greeted with a jaunty "Good morning, gentlemen of the press." The twins quite freely answered questions, other than those relating to the crime, but a comment by Ray was particularly revealing: "The one thing that unnerved me was when my wife came to the police station (Steubenville) to bid me good-bye. She held my boy up for me to kiss and he held out his little hands for me to take him. When he saw the bars, my soul sank to zero."

That afternoon (June 21), Hugh's case was submitted to the jury. Only one ballot was needed on the question of Hugh's guilt or innocence, followed by another as to what the penalty should be. One hour and 24 minutes after retiring, the twelve jurors returned to the courtroom, with the foreman announcing a verdict of murder in the first degree and a sentence of life imprisonment in the Oregon State Penitentiary. Neither Mr. nor Mrs. DeAutremont were present for Hugh's sentencing, or later, when Ray and Roy were sentenced.

During the trial, Attorney Collier had approached the Post Office Inspectors and the Southern Pacific Special Agents, offering to have Hugh plead guilty to a charge of manslaughter, with the understanding that a sentence of 10 years be given. The offer was bluntly refused, as there was an almost fraternal relationship among railroad employees, and the vicious, senseless murder of four fellow workers had created violent hostility among the railroad people against the perpetrators of the crimes. Also, with the mountain of evidence, even though it was mostly of a circumstantial nature, the prosecution was quite certain of a conviction.

While Ray and Roy had both entered pleas of not guilty upon being arraigned, several "off the record" meetings were held in an effort to save the expense of further trials. Also, on the evening of Hugh's sentencing, Judge Thomas met with the Post Office people and representatives of Southern Pacific, and stated that, after hearing all the testimony and having viewed the evidence at Hugh's trial, he did not believe any jury procurable in the State of Oregon would ever hang Roy and Ray upon the circumstantial evidence available. And, in his opinion, if the boys were willing to make a full and complete confession and plead guilty, with the understanding they would be sentenced to life imprisonment, their pleas should be accepted and stipulated sentences imposed. This was finally agreed to by the prosecution, the defense council and the two accused young men. It was further agreed that none of the remaining indictments would be dismissed, so if any of the three were ever released, they could be immediately brought to trial on the outstanding charges.

Inspectors C. W. B. Long and Tennyson Jefferson, accompanied by Newton Chaney and George W. Neilson, Deputy District Attorney together with Sheriff Jennings, went to the jail and spent the night of June 21 taking the detailed confessions of Roy and Ray. On June 23, all three of the accused men signed the various confessions, which cleared up some of the doubts which had been lingering in the minds of many people. It certainly relieved the nagging consciences of several members of the jury.

Ironically, Dan O'Connell, the dogged chief of the Southern Pacific special agents, whose persistent efforts continued unflaggingly from the day of the crime until the capture of all three suspects, was not able to be at the trial. He was quite ill and at Byron Hot Springs for treatment, but it is certain that he intently followed all published reports of the capture and trial of the criminals, the pursuit of whom he had helped to spearhead throughout the world.

Otis Skinner, the noted actor, had been in Medford on June 20 and later, while appearing at the Helig Theatre in Portland, endeavored to capitalize on the publicity of the trial by issuing an observation that Hugh DeAutremont should have been an actor, with his tremendous sense of the dramatic, commenting on Hugh's statements after being sentenced, in particular his, "My God! That bell! I thought it would drive me crazy."

A forlornly tragic footnote was subsequently written by young Jack Vick, who had returned to his home in Arkansas following Hugh's sentencing. He later left Arkansas to visit Hugh in the penitentiary and, while trying to grab hold of a freight car at Vian, Oklahoma, slipped and fell, and was fatally injured. The youth's dying request to the hospital attendants was to please notify his friend Hugh of his plight, and referred to Hugh as, "The best boy I ever knew; I loved him as a brother . . . he was wonderful to me."

Chapter 14

A Young Mother and Child

While in the Steubenville jail, the twins, expecting to be hanged, provided a great cover-up for their deep-rooted concern about the future and delighted throngs of curiosity seekers gathered outside by singing lively songs. But, despite their bravado, they were filled with remorse for the troubles they had caused to people. Ray, for instance, commented that, "My mistake was in marrying Hazel. My wife is the finest little girl you ever met. I shouldn't have married a girl like that. I should have married someone who wouldn't care and one that I wouldn't care so much about. As it is, here I am leaving a young and splendid girl all alone with her baby in a strange town. She can't and won't understand." During this time, he obtained a copy of one of the many pictures being taken of him and sent it to Hazel, inscribed, "To my loving wife Hazel. Because I love you. Take good care of Jack. God bless your parents. [Signed] Ray Charles DeAutremont."

The young mother was stunned and unbelieving as the police arrested Ray and drove off to jail with him. And the words of her suspicious neighbor came back to haunt her, the one who had cautioned her before the wedding, "Hazel, you'd better think it over. I know everyone is crazy about those boys, and you're in love with Elmer, but, remember, they came from a far way off. Maybe they're in some sort of trouble."

When first jailed Roy had thrown the ring he was wearing into a tank. It was Hugh's class ring and initialed H.A.D. Later he told Chief of Police Ross Cunningham, "You've been good to me. I slipped off a ring when you arrested me and threw it in a tank in the jail. You may have it. "Cunningham had the tank taken apart and salvaged the ring.

On June 17, the twins were manacled and, in company with Jackson County (Oregon) Sheriff Jennings and five other law officers, boarded the train for Oregon. Hazel (Goodwin) DeAutremont had disposed of those possessions which couldn't be taken with her and had sorrowfully returned with her baby to her parents' home in Hanging Rock, arriving there on June 11.

Dapper Roy and Ray at the railroad depot in Steubenville, Ohio, with Sheriff Jennings and unidentified law enforcement officers.

Initially, her family was extremely bitter towards Ray and the public tragedy he had brought to their daughter. Mrs. Sprouse sadly watched Hazel, who sat day after day rocking and crying, holding baby Jackie Hugh tightly. Her blunt, but ignored, advice was for Hazel to forget Ray.

Her parents' bitterness soon mellowed somewhat, for they had truly liked their son-in-law and, obviously, their daughter loved him. Hazel carefully followed every line of the newspaper accounts about the case in far-off Oregon, hoping against hope that some

Hazel DeAutremont and Jackie Hugh came from Ohio to visit Ray in prison.

miracle of miracles would bring back her beloved husband. She wrote faithfully to Ray and fretted that she wasn't nearer so she could visit him in prison. Sad letters from Ray tore at her heart strings, as he reaffirmed his love and questioned whether he could stand being separated from her and the baby without losing his sanity.

Although she carefully hoarded the few hundred dollars Ray and Roy had given her, it was rapidly slipping away and she realized, once it was gone, there would be great difficulty in again accumulating enough to pay her way to see Ray. Despite the fact that her relatives had strongly urged her not to go see him, towards the latter part of July, she realized there was only $97.00 left and suddenly decided she must go then or never. Slipping away from those who might try to dissuade her, she bought a day-coach ticket to Eugene, Oregon.

By carefully husbanding the remaining few dollars, she and the baby managed to eat during the 2,500 mile trip but, when she arrived in Eugene, there was only 47¢ left. The taxi fare to her father-in-law's home was 50¢ but a cooperative taxi driver laughingly accepted the 47¢ and dropped her off there, unexpected and un-

known, except by name. It certainly must have taken considerable
courage for the inexperienced, young girl from the hills to have un-
dertaken such a venture. But, fortunately, the young are blessed
with great optimism.

Even though Paul was thrilled to meet his daughter-in-law and
see his grandson, he was reluctant to take her to visit the boys in
prison. Since the trial, the thought of their crimes had shrouded
him in brooding shame and he had refused to visit them. Hazel,
however, was extremely anxious to visit her prisoner husband and
defiantly replied to questions, "I'm not sorry I married Ray. I'm
glad. He was good to me and I love him. The two years we lived
together were the happiest of my life. You say he hid his identity
from me. You're wrong. I knew the real Ray. You knew the crazy
one who committed that crime."

Soon learning of her presence, the reporters descended upon the
little wife and mother to throw a barrage of relevant and irrelevant
questions at her. Laughing, the pretty little country girl would toss
her head proudly, wrinkle her slightly freckled nose and frankly reply to the questions. Throughout all her answers rang the obvious
fact that she dearly loved her husband, and, while she was very
sorry for the crime he had committed, she in no way regretted having married him.

After several days of becoming acquainted with her in-laws and
discussing a visit with the three boys, she persuaded Paul to borrow
a car and, on the Wednesday following her arrival, he took Hazel
and the baby to visit Ray.

On the way to the prison, Paul bared the grinding bitterness in
his soul, as he urged, "Hazel, don't be a fool. Go away some place
with the baby. Change your name of DeAutremont. It's ruined.
There's a stigma attached to it that will follow you to the grave." In
reply to these virulent complaints about the ignominy of it all, and
the disgrace to the name of DeAutremont, she would not bend an
inch, merely cradling her baby tighter in her arms and replying,
"What does a name mean anyway?"

The boys were overjoyed at the visit. They sat on one side of a
long table, with Hazel, Paul and baby Jackie Hugh on the other
side. The guards thoughtfully stood some distance away. The baby
was passed from boy to boy, each striving to make it laugh the
most. Ray's pride in his child was most obvious. He told Hazel that
he would begin working shortly in the flax-seed plant and would
then be paid $15 per month, which he would have sent to her for ex-
penses. She broke the news that he was to be a father again, in
February.

By November, the little mountain girl was uncomfortable with
her second child and becoming homesick for home and family.
While, initially, she had had a fine relationship with the
DeAutremonts, this was badly deteriorating, for Paul did not want

to visit his sons in prison and Hazel's presence was a constant and abrasive reminder of the infamous situation in which the family found itself. Also, she prefered to be with her immediate family for the child's birth. Her father sent the money for her return.

In February 1928, she wrote Ray of the birth of his second son, whom she defiantly and proudly named Ray.

Throughout the following years, Hazel faithfully wrote Ray. She told him of the progress of his two sons, cheerfully encouraged him, and prayed the severity of his sentence would be reduced. But, as the years passed, the gallant young girl, with the laughing eyes and indomitable spirit, slowly began to have her faith eroded. The great distance between them and her inability to finance visits began to draw a film of forgetfulness over the past and those all-too-few months of memories.

Hazel, eventually, resigned herself to the fact Ray would probably never be released. The obvious animosity of many people in high places was more than her love, at a distance, could conquer. And, even though numerous people were striving to assist the boys in obtaining paroles, in particular for Hugh, hopes faded of any success, and Ray's chances appeared even less likely.

With each passing year, the exercise in futility sapped more of the vitality of her dreams, eventually becoming more than even her staunch spirit could withstand. Letters became less and less frequent. Finally, after a quarter-century of waiting, she obtained a divorce (which Ray had often urged) and remarried. Nevertheless, she had certainly proven herself as a sturdily loyal wife during her long years of waiting.

The author visited the former Hazel DeAutremont in her modest home, only a short distance from where she and Ray lived as newlyweds. She still speaks with affection of the man she has not seen for almost half a century. While widowed for several years, her living room is ringed with pictures of her family. Jackie Hugh is a fine-looking, middle-aged man, with a very responsible position in a near-by plant and thoroughly respected in the community.

Ray Jr. was a veteran of the Korean War and, apparently, was never able to readjust to a return to civilian life. One can easily conject that the darker aspects of the DeAutremont mystique may also have been in force, eventually driving him to his suicide.

Chapter 15

End of The Line

On June 27, 1927, the three new prisoners reported for work in the prison's lime plant. Ray and Roy were to push wheelbarrows, with Hugh assigned to a somewhat lighter task. Later, Roy was shifted to shoveling sawdust at the prison heating plant and, still later, he was assigned to the prison barber shop where for many years he practiced his first profession, without going blind as he had once feared. Ray was eventually transferred to the prison flax mill.

In a rather sensitive and thoughtful gesture, the prison officials did put the twins as cellmates.

One can only speculate as to the remorseful thoughts which must have gone through the minds of the three young men as they found themselves within the walls of the penitentiary. Perhaps they felt they were fortunate not to have been sentenced to death . . . and, with the inborn confidence of youth, assumed they would be released on parole within a few years.

Shortly after the three brothers entered the Penitentiary rumors began circulating that they would soon be paroled. There was no such thought in the minds of responsible authorities in view of the enormity of the crime committed, as reflected by the following letter.

Medford
December 18th, 1929

Mr. Tennyson Jefferson,
Post Office Inspector,
Medford, Oregon.

Dear Sir:-

Relative to our conversation concerning a report that I had circulated, or was circulating, a petition for the parole of the DeAutremont brothers, now serving a life sentence in the State penitentiary at Salem, Oregon for the murder of four men in the Siskiyou train robbery, I would state that I have never circulated or seen any petition for the parole of these bandits and the report above referred to is false in every particular. Shortly after the first of July of this year I received a form from the Warden of the penitentiary for a statement from me as to whether or not I would

The Oregon State Penitentiary at Salem was the home of the three DeAutremonts for decades to follow.

RAY DE AUTREMONT

Oregon State Penitentiary,Salem,Oregon
Received from Jackson County 6-24-27
Crime: Murder,First Degree: Life
Age: 27 in 1927
Complexion: Medium
Eyes: Light Reddish Brown
Weight: 123.
Height: 5 feet 6 inches
Build:Slight.
Native Arkansas,French-German Descent.
Round blotch scar about ¼ size of dime
on right cheek; pit scar under left jaw;
two boil scars back of neck,upper front
tooth is missing; left great toe nail de-
formed.

ROY DE AUTREMONT

Oregon State Penitentiary,Salem,Oregon.
Received from Jackson County 6-24-27
Crime: Murder,First Degree. Life.
Age 27 in 1927
Complexion: Medium
Eyes: Light redding Brown;
Hair: Light brown
Weight 127
Height: 5 feet 5 inches
Build: Slight
Native Arkansas - German-French descent.
Small mole on right cheek; brown scar on
outside calf of right leg; round boil scar
on right buttock; six round boil scars on
left leg above knee.

HUGH DE AUTREMONT
Oregon State Penitentiary,Salem,Ore.
Received from Jackson County,6-24-27
Crime: Murder,First Degree, Life
Age: 23 in 1927   Hair:Light Brown
Complexion: Light   Weight: 125 lbs
Eyes: Blue   Build:Small
Native:Arkansas. French-German Descent
Little finger left hand curved inward;
round scar back of right hand; large
oval scar inside right wrist;round scar
right side back head; two round scars
on right groin.

The photos taken at the Oregon State Penitentiary ended the stream of pictures
which had been decorating public places for more than three years.

be in favor of paroling the DeAutremonts. This was merely a form letter sent out by the Warden on all prisoners for whom he did not have such a report. I returned the form with the statement that I would have absolutely nothing to do with paroling these men and that I was most bitterly opposed to any step in that direction. The court also received a form similar to the one sent me and he likewise sent it back with a similar endorsement.

My only regret is that these men could not have been given the extreme penalty. I shall never be in favor of their parole.

Very truly yours,

Ralph G. Jennings
Sheriff of Jackson County, Oregon

RGJ/oea

Over the years, the prisoners' optimism slowly lost its glow, as decade after decade came and went. They were all intelligent, sensitive men, and the mental as well as physical restrictions of imprisonment were undoubtedly terribly depressing. Too, in the 1920's and early 1930's the prison was a very rough place, for big, tough, mean convicts pretty generally ran things inside. There were some rebellious periods from Roy and Ray and they, occasionally, did get tossed into "the cage", a miserable situation of being literally inside an open cage, near the old front wall. So-called "hard cases" were thrown into these limited confines to stay, rain or shine, in an effort to soften them.

Eventually, Ray accepted the situation and began making the most of what was available and worthwhile. But, he stayed mostly to himself and generally spoke only when spoken to. He continued to read a great deal and, actually, became quite a well-educated person, able to speak and read several languages, later teaching Spanish and French in prison classes. A number of years after entering prison, he became interested in painting and, through the help of other inmates having a bit of painting knowledge, he became a proficient primitive painter. He copied many scenes from magazines, such as the National Geographic, and these paintings were frequently sold at the prison hobby shop.

Initially, Roy was the best able to adjust to confinement and his cheerfulness was a great boon to his brothers. However, by the late 1940's, the gradual loss of hope and plaguing remorse for a wasted life began to ravage his mind. He turned morose and argumentative; even Ray had great trouble getting along with him. Eventually, the two were separated, but Roy's condition continued to worsen and in the Fall of 1949 he went beserk, virtually destroying the interior of his cell. Doctors diagnosed him as schizophrenic and transferred him to the State Hospital for the Insane. Shortly thereafter he was given a prefontal lobotomy operation. It was not totally successful but it did have a calming effect on him. Many

Ray DeAutremont became an accomplished primitive artist and sold many of his paintings at the prison shop. This is one owned by the author.

years earlier he had worked at the institution as an attendant and one wonders if, in his rational moments, he belabored the strange twist of fate which returned him there.

Belle DeAutremont sold her Lakewood, N.M. home and store, and moved to Salem to be near her sons. She operated a rooming house for many years, although dinner was generally late on Thursday evenings, for that was her afternoon to visit them. She almost lost the property once, when she fell behind in her mortgage payments, but was saved by Hugh, who gave her $1,000 he had slowly saved over the years.

The author had the opportunity to be acquainted with a man who served time with Ray in an adjacent cell during the 1950's. He had great praise for Ray, stating that while, by then, he had become a rather typical-looking convict, short, balding and heavy-necked, he was thoroughly respected by both convicts and guards. For years, he had been confined to the old cell block "B", a cold water cell, and even when more modern cell blocks were built with hot water and a modern toilet, requested permission to remain there and was allowed to do so.

In the mid-1950's, a violent three-day riot racked the prison, which was finally put down by the guards, with the assistance of the Oregon National Guard. There was much shooting and a great deal of damage, but neither of the DeAutremonts was involved or harmed, although they did lose some of their privileges, as did other prisoners.

A year or so after Hugh, prisoner #9902, entered prison, he was moved from the lime plant to the laundry, where he worked until

1933. At that point, he was transferred to the print shop. That same year he also became interested in writing and took three courses in English and Writing from the University of Oregon. Three years later, he created the award-winning prison newspaper *The Shadows,* for which he wrote all the editorials until 1939. Ray also frequently wrote articles for the publication. In addition, the shop printed *The Oregon Pulse,* and commercial cards, and handled other job printing. Hugh soon became a skilled typographer and linotypist. In fact, the statement was made by a man, aware of Hugh's extensive efforts in the print shop, that the State couldn't afford to let Hugh be paroled, as it would lose too much in the way of printing revenues.

Although continually optimistic about his eventual parole, Hugh was well aware of the strong opposition he faced from the Post Office people and railroad employees. In March 1940, prison psychiatrist, Dr. John W. Evans, issued a psychiatric report highly complimentary of Hugh, commenting that he was "of good physique, placid, stable temperament, marked drive and energy, superior intelligence and well formed personal and social habits . . . maintains an anxious, realistic attitude toward the possibility of his return to society . . . He is a good parole risk . . . He is well equipped to live an average middle-class existence . . ." However, he was not considered for parole that year.

On September 14, 1941, Dr. Evans again stated "It is my opinion that the facts of his 1940 and 1941 status depict him as a candidate for parole consideration." (See appendix, Dr. Evans' letter, dated September 8, 1947.)

Dr. Robert A. Coen, prison psychiatrist, reported on April 26, 1949, "This man is highly intelligent . . . From a psychiatric standpoint, it is considered this man presents a reasonably good parole risk." (See appendix, letter of Dr. Robert A. Coen dated April 26, 1949.) Again, there was no recommendation for parole, in view of the outstanding charges, still threatening, should he be released.

Numerous interested citizens were doing everything possible to get Hugh released on parole. Letters from many prominent people were received by the Governor and other state officials, on his behalf. In 1943, Major Donald E. Mathes, of Headquarters, 14th Battalion, Armored Forces Replacement Training Center, Fort Knox, Kentucky, offered to have him as a soldier in his battalion. (See appendix, letter of Major Donald E. Mathes, dated June 1, 1943.)

Mrs. Edward C. Kelly, who, as Miss Mary Greiner, a reporter for the Medford *Daily News* covering his trial, endeavored for years to get Hugh considered for parole. (See appendix, Mrs. Edward C. Kelly's letter dated November 16, 1948.) Her husband, the late Judge Edward C. Kelly, materially assisted in her dedicated efforts.

One by one, the more implacable opponents to a parole for Hugh died, or mellowed with advancing years. On January 3, 1948, at the age of 73, one of the major resisters to any parole, Southern Pacific agent Don O'Connell, died. He had persistently fought any attempt to release the men on parole, although he did visit them several times and was friendly with them.

In September, 1950, when a hearing on a parole application for Hugh was finally set, it was violently opposed by Attorney General George Neuner and Jackson County District Attorney George Neilson. Mr. Neuner obdurately announced, "I will oppose any application for parole of these brothers as long as I live . . . I consider the crime in which these brothers were involved among the most serious in the criminal annals of this state." Mr. Neilson had said on August 17, 1950, anticipating the hearing, "As long as I am District Attorney, the three indictments will be prosecuted if Hugh DeAutremont should be released."

By 1951, it appeared the public sympathy was overwhelmingly in favor of Hugh being paroled, but the Southern Pacific people and Post Office officials were adamant against any breach of the 1927 agreement, under which the various outstanding indictments had been held in abeyance.

On November 14, 1951 when, seemingly, public sentiment had reached a more temperate state and that there might be a parole hearing for Hugh, Post Office Department official Tennyson Jefferson, Inspector in Charge, together with F. W. Wood, Post Office Inspector, directed a joint eighteen page letter to Paul W. Haviland, Jackson County prosecuting attorney, stating:

Dear Sir:

Reference is made to our conference with you at Medford on July 23 and 24, 1951, relating to the above-named defendants (referring to Hugh DeAutremont, Roy A. DeAutremont and Ray Charles DeAutremont). You will recall that a full discussion of the case was had; that, although these men were convicted on an additional murder indictment, Docket No. 629-C, and are presently serving life sentences in the Oregon State Penitentiary, efforts have been made from time to time to effect their release and undoubtedly such efforts will be continued in the future; that the Postmaster General, Chief Post Office Inspector and all others in the Postal Service, Officials of the Southern Pacific Railroad, Engineers, Firemen and Trainmen's Unions, and others, including Mr. George Neuner, Attorney General for the State of Oregon, and the United States Attorney for Oregon, are opposed to the release of these criminals and are firmly convinced that if they do not spend the rest of their natural lives in confinement for the atrocious, cold blooded murders they committed, the ends of justice will have failed. You assured us that in the event these men, or any of them, are ever released, that you will immediately proceed to prosecute one or more of the outstanding indictments. Etc., etc.

The lengthy letter proceded to detail the entire case with a recap of the crime and a list of the witnesses who were still available for prosecution of the outstanding indictments.

Hugh sardonically commented on the periodic visits by Southern Pacific Special Agents, suggesting they merely dropped by to make certain the infamous DeAutremonts were being appropriately treated and not about to be paroled.

Chapter 16

Paroled at Last

On January 9, 1959, the 55-year-old Hugh was finally paroled from the Oregon State Penitentiary, after having served more than 31 years. It was a rainy day. He stood in a protected area to keep his new, light-brown suit dry, and chatted with reporters. The slighty-built, aging man, touched at the temples with gray, told the newsmen that he just wanted to find a job in a printing shop and live in obscurity. "I've had all the publicity I need," he said.

Reporters talked to others who had known Hugh. Deputy Warden Gregory Boyd said Hugh was a model prisoner. "He was as reliable as a hired worker. Society has received its pound of flesh," he added.

During those many years following the trial in Jacksonville, the three men, Hugh in particular, had made a host of friends. Mary Greiner had befriended Hugh when she covered his trial in 1927, as a reporter for the Medford *Daily News.* This friendship continued through the long period of his imprisonment. Subsequently, she married Edward Kelly, an attorney and later Circuit Judge, who also assisted over the years in trying to get Hugh pardoned, which would, in turn, pave the way for the twins.

The long crusade of the Kelly family, as well as many others, was finally rewarded, but only following the efforts of their daughter, Noreen Kelly, also an attorney. Miss Kelly had graduated from the University of Oregon Law School in 1955 and, after the passage of a State law, somewhat tailor-made for the DeAutremonts' case, she arranged to have Hugh plead guilty to one of the outstanding murder indictments. Hugh received another life sentence and the remaining murder indictments were dismissed.

Miss Kelly and Attorney George W. Friede, of Portland, had Hugh plead guilty to the one remaining charge of assaulting a federal mail clerk, for which a sentence of 5 years probation was levied, and the last great obstacle to Hugh's parole was removed.

Many of the friends and co-workers of the slain men, from so long before, had died or became less vindictive with the passing of time and no concerted efforts were made to block the parole, although there were some bitter comments from a few unforgetting and unforgiving old-timers. Friede made an impassioned statement: "If society is to encourage the rehabilitation of criminals, it cannot say to one, 'No, your crime is too terrible. We are going to deny you what we offer to others.'"

Mrs. Claire Argow, executive secretary of the Oregon Prison Association, described Hugh as, "One of the best inmates any institution could have . . . parolees at my office seldom speak of former prison associates, with one exception; 'Little Hughie", as he is known in penitentiary parlance. He is an immense power for good inside the prison and I know he will continue a worthwhile life outside."

Upon release from prison, it was arranged for Hugh to go to San Francisco, where he was placed under the jurisdiction of the California parole system, as it was felt his opportunities there would be considerably greater. His parole officer would not permit him to go to work immediately, considering it essential for him to get the feel of supervised freedom; to accept and familiarize himself with new surroundings and conditions after so many years of restricted activity.

An inexpensive hotel room was obtained for him in downtown San Francisco and, each day, he would take long walks, looking in store windows, getting acquainted with unfamiliar objects, passing homes and people on the streets. He was just learning to look again and each day reported the experience to his parole officer and discussed this new pattern of life.

In 1947, while working at the penitentiary printing shop, Hugh had met a young woman. Eventually, they fell in love and had kept in touch, as much as his confinement would permit, hoping that in time things might possibly work out for them. With his release, marriage was planned but, under the terms of his parole, it was necessary, to wait 60 days before the wedding could take place. Also, he wished to be working prior to being married, and a residence requirement of the Union made it necessary to wait 30 days before he could join. While anxious for these restrictive periods to pass, after 31 years of waiting, he had learned to wait.

Hugh applied for a job at one of the metropolitan newspapers as a linotype operator and, subject to obtaining membership in the Union, he was hired. The Parole Office had advised Hugh not to mention his background to the Union business agent, but, when it seemed the business agent was reluctant to accept him, questioning, "How come you never bothered to join our Union before? You're not young. You claim all this experience . . ." Hugh's hopes began to fade and finally, in desperation, he softly blurted out "Take a look at my name."

"Oh . . . of course," the agent said and his recognition quickly turned to compassion and an immediate acceptance into the Union.

No further questions were asked and a few days later Hugh reported for work.

After only six days on the job on February 14, Hugh was stricken with a sudden, stabbing abdominal pain and was admitted to San Francisco General Hospital, where a series of tests were begun. On March 11, minor exploratory surgery was performed and it was discoverd he had an incurable cancer.

Each day the still pretty woman, no longer quite so young, who had patiently waited a long 12 years for Hugh, visited the hospital and talked with him. Plans were discussed for their future — plans which both really knew would never transpire—but, as with all sensitive persons, things become so much easier when a little honest pretense is involved. Both of them knew that an unforgiving fate had again cruelly intervened in Hugh's life and there would be no marriage or future for him.

A full circle in time resulted when the *Medford Mail Tribune* assigned Mary (Greiner) Kelly to go to San Francisco and interview Hugh, as she had so many times since that day in March of 1927, when the handsome, smiling, optimistic young man had arrived in the stately old Jacksonville Courthouse for trial. The aging, hopelessly-ill Hugh talked freely to his long-time friend, exhibiting little of the resentfulness which must have been in his heart, as this last, tiny chance for a bit of happiness was being ruthlessly snatched away, just when it was within his grasp.

Hugh never left the hospital alive. At 1:30 a.m. Sunday, March 30, 1959, he died of cancer. He was buried at Belcrest Memorial Park, in Salem, Oregon, beside the grave of his mother, Belle DeAutremont.

On October 26, 1961, 61-year-old Ray was finally paroled, the path having been cleared by Hugh. Ray remained in Oregon, quietly working as a custodian at the University of Oregon, endeavoring to avoid the notoriety which plagued him for too many years. In November 1972, he was granted one of his great hopes "to be a free man before I die," as Governor Tom McCall commuted his 2 consecutive life terms. Ray stated, "You can't imagine how wonderful it feels to be free and not have an invisible chain around you that somebody can pull whenever they want to", and summed his many years in prison, "It's amazing how little you remember. The routine of prison acts like an eraser on the mind. What is left is just a blurred memory of days and days and days and days."

At the time of this writing (1977) Roy is still confined to the State mental hospital in Salem, regarded as harmless, but hopelessly insane, interested mostly in eating and playing billiards.

In 1973, the long silence of Ray DeAutremont was broken when he was persuaded to participate in an hour-long documentary on KGW-TV in Portland, Oregon. Entitled "DeAutremont—The Train Robber—The Man." The program re-examined the story of the holdup through the eyes of Ray. For the first time since 1923, he revisited the scene of his debacle. He also had a poignant visit with Roy at the State hospital, although it made virtually no impression on the twin brother with whom he had shared such a long and terrible closeness. It was the first time he had seen Roy since 1949.

About the same time as the TV special, the *Oregon Journal* (Portland) ran a series of twelve feature articles by Jack Pement, reviewing the historic crime and featuring current interviews with the old, train hold up man.

In 1973, Ray had a slight stroke, but recovered. He still lives a rather quiet life in a very modest home in Eugene (1977) but appears to be relishing some of his new found status as a celebrity; autographs are grandly given.

The tragic blight which hung over the three unfortunate brothers is about ended, and while the author in no way condones the brutally terrible crime they committed, he feels that something of an injustice has probably taken place. Their actions, over many years, bore out Professor Heinrich's analysis of so long ago, when he stated that, in his opinion, they were not criminally inclined and, undoubtedly, this would be the single criminal act during their lifetime.

Had these three very young men lived at another time or, perhaps, even another place, undoubtedly they would have been fine citizens, effectively contributing to their community. A slight stature, coupled with a great deal of family instability, together with a period of depression and considerable social unrest, combined to make them vulnerable to a situation. It was the witch hunt that took place in the State of Washington, in an effort to destroy the feared I.W.W. which caught the impressionable young and idealistic Ray. A year's imprisonment at the Washington State Reformatory threw him in with a group of young criminals, triggering a twisted reaction taking more time to recover from than he had. For, by the time he had overcome this resentful, embittered viewpoint, it was too late; he and his brothers had been dragged into a desperately hopeless maelstrom of crime and guilt, virtually destroying their lives.

In addition to the ruined lives of the three brothers, the lives of four innocent trainmen were snuffed out with immeasurable heartache and discomfort to their families. Other members of the DeAutremont family suffered great agonies. Ray's young wife faithfully waited for many years before losing hope and finally remarrying. Ray's two sons were faced with the fact their father was a notorious criminal and an inmate of a prison for murder. The death of young Jack Vick was indirectly a result of his friendship for Hugh. Family, sweethearts, wife, children, friends, relatives . . . all swept into years of agony. embarrassment and sorrow from one terrible crime, spawned in the twisted bitterness of Ray's resentment and followed by a single, stupid, panic-filled, brutal portion of October 11, 1923, on a quiet mountain top in Southern Oregon.

It was really too bad, for the boys were all capable of so much better things than the star-crossed lives they led. Unfortunately, regrets have never been able to alter the past.

the end

Appendix

The lack of multitudinous footnotes throughout this book has been deliberate. I do not personally enjoy switching my attention back and forth, and in this instance I felt they would not materially contribute to the story. I would like to emphasize that all dialogue quotations were from printed sources and not from my imagination; as a student of history I do not appreciate dreamed-up accounts of what might or might not have been said by someone.

Numerous documents and sources were used in accumulating the information for this book. Some of these items were in compact form which I felt would provide an interesting adjunct and give additional flavor to the overall picture of the crime. Only the confession of Ray has been included for it was felt that he had been the Pied Piper to the brothers' crime.

The letter from Mrs. Kelly is merely a representative of uncountable similar letters, but due to the unflagging interest and assistance of the Kelly family, the author felt it justly due of recognition.

Ray DeAutremont's Confession

I, Ray DeAutremont, after having been fully advised of my constitutional rights and legal rights under the laws of the State of Oregon, to the effect that I do not have to make a statement, and that any statement that I may make can and will be used against me and after due and deliberate consideration, without duress or coercion, knowing the consequences of my statements, I voluntarily make the following statement concerning my connection with the holdup of the first section of Southern Pacific train No. 13 on October 11th, 1923, at Tunnel No. 13, Jackson County, Oregon.

That the idea of making some robbery first occurred to me while I was confined in the Washington State Reformatory at Monroe, Wash. where I was given a sentence of one year for criminal syndicalism in 1919-1920. The robbery of a train on the Southern Pacific Railway was first planned by me in the summer of 1923, I had a big crime in mind, however, early in 1923, when I visited New Mexico, at which time I talked the matter over with Hugh and put him in the frame of mind for joining with me in the commission of such a crime. I had already talked the matter over with Roy DeAutremont before going to New Mexico. When I left New Mexico, it was the understanding that Hugh DeAutremont would come up to Oregon later in the spring when we would work out a plan for a big robbery and get sufficient money together to finance it, it being understood that Hugh, Roy and myself would carry out this robbery. Hugh came up in June, 1923, and went to work with myself and Roy at Silverton, Oregon, with the Silver Falls Lumber Company. I might state that to the best of my recollection, that when I went to New Mexico, over the Southern Pacific, I gave thought to what might be the best place to hold up a train.

We carefully thought out in a general way the crime we had in mind and in September, 1923, we visited and looked over the country from Portland to Northern California with the idea of finding the best place to hold up a Southern Pacific train. We decided that the best place was the Siskiyou Mountains and that train No. 13 was the best train to hold up, the one that would most likely have a large amount of money on it.

We three boys, Roy, Hugh and myself, went to Portland, Oregon in the early part of September, 1923, purchased a Nash automobile to be used if found practicable, in making our get away after the robbery. We stole a detonator, wire and dynamite near Oregon City, shortly after the car was purchased, having already purchased camping supplies and drove the car to Eugene, Oregon, and at Eugene we bought most of our provisions for cache to be made, stayed around home for a few days and on or about Sept. 18th, 1923, the three of us left Eugene, Ore. in the Nash automobile with provisions and camping outfit, telling our father that we were going on a camping trip up in the Puget Sound country.

We went directly to the Siskiyou Mountains about a quarter of a mile from the summit of the mountain, turned off the road about 300 feet from the road and camped, the automobile being concealed from the Pacific Highway. We stayed at this location about one week and then moved to what is known as Camp No. 2, remaining there several days trying out the detonating machine and doing considerable target practice and studying the topography of the country. While at this camp it was decided that we would burn up the tarpaulin used as a tent, Hugh's wooden tool chest, and various other things that might lead to our identification. I do not know whether it was three or four days or a week that we stayed at Mt. Crest cabin, and therefore, cannot state positively how long we were at Camp No. 2. The latter part of September, 1923, it was decided that Hugh should return in the Nash car to father at Eugene, for the reason that it could not be used in making our get away. It was intended that if successful in the robbery that I would go to Eugene and get this car, come back and get my brothers and make our escape. Hugh ran into a cow on the Siskiyou Mountains and had to stay in Ashland until his car was repaired, this naturally made Hugh late in returning. He finally returned to us at Camp No. 2, about Sept. 30th, 1923.

During this period we had prepared a cache in which to hide and into which to take the loot we expected to obtain remaining there until I could proceed to Eugene and obtain the Nash automobile in which to make our getaway.

October 11th, 1923, was the date decided upon for the robbery. About 12:00 Noon on this date, we took our equipment to the south end of the tunnel, consisting of detonating machine, three pack sacks, three foot pads (sets), a one lb. can of pepper, guns, flashlights, etc. The detonating machine was wrapped in a pair of blue overalls. We laid out our dynamite, about thirty feet from the entrance of the tunnel, connected the wire, and placed the detonating machine and Hugh and Roy started for the north entrance, going through the tunnel while I remained at the south entrance, smoking cigarettes. It was the understanding that Hugh and Roy would board the tank of engine when the train slowed down at the north entrance to test brakes. The train came through and the engine was just starting out the south entrance when it came to a stop. At this time Roy was on the back end of the oil tank, Hugh was in the cab with the engineer and fireman, I was beside the dynamite inside the tunnel and handed the dynamite up to Roy. Before I did this I noticed the mail clerk stick his head out the side door of the mail car and I attempted to shoot him with a shot gun I had. Roy and I went up to the engine cab and Hugh made the fireman and engineer get down on the right hand side at the gangway of engine. We drove them up clear of the front end of the tunnel, where they would be safe from debris, Roy gave the detonator a push and the mouth of the tunnel was filled with smoke, as the result of the explosion of the charge of dynamite, which had been placed against the front door of the mail car. Roy then took the fireman and started back to uncouple the mail car. The gases were too much for the fireman and Roy sent him back. The fireman and engineer were covered by Hugh and myself and in a few seconds I saw someone coming with a red light on the right hand side of the train. (I later found that this was the brakeman Roy had sent forward to have the engine move the mail car ahead). I shot at this man with the red light with my shot gun and at the same time Hugh shot him with his .45 Colt, the man staggered up to me and muttered "that other fellow said to pull the thing ahead" so far as I could make out. I seen he was dying and either Hugh or I shot him again.

The engineer was standing on the ground during this time and Hugh put him back up into the cab and told him to pull the mail car ahead, and he attempted to do so a number of times, but the engine wheels merely spun around and he failed to move same. Hugh then put the engineer back on the ground beside the fireman while Roy and I looked the thing over to see what could be done with a view to uncoupling the mail car and engine, but we found conditions such that we knew we could not move either. Roy and I went back to the mail car and entered same through the front end but our flash lights would not cut the steam and smoke and we shortly thereafter left the mail car, knowing that we were helpless in the matter, as the steam and smoke would not clear up for half an hour or more. When we got back on the ground, Hugh in the meantime having ordered the engineer back into the cab, we walked a few paces toward the front of the tunnel, and met the fireman standing alongside the engine tank, with his arms in the air, at which time Roy and I held a brief consultation as to what ought to be done. We decided to kill the fireman and Roy shot him twice, with his .45 Colt, I climbed up on the engine step, and looked in the cab, where Hugh had the engineer covered on the left side of the gangway, and I shouted at him to bump him off and lets clear out of here immediately after which Hugh shot the engineer in the head with his .45 Colt. We then fled to our cache, which was located between two and three miles northwest of the south entrance of the tunnel.

The above statement is made as aforesaid without duress or coercion and is signed in the presence of the witnesses whose names appear hereon and I have read the statement and know fully the contents of same, and I have been treated with courtesy and kind consideration by the officials who have taken the above statement.

s/s Ray Chas. D'Autremont

Witnesses: Subscribed and sworn to before me by
                                   the above named Ray Chas. DeAutremont
G. W. Neilson   this 23rd day of June, 1927
O. W. Dunford
A. W. Deming
J. O. Cave   s/s W. J. Looker
Tennyson Jefferson   Notary Public for Oregon
Newton C. Chaney   My Commission Expires July 12, 1930.

(note: the punctuation and sentence structures of the confession has been reproduced just as it was in the original document with the only editorial changes being the correction of several obviously typographically misspelled words.)

Letter to the Parole Board on behalf of
Hugh DeAutremont . . . dated June 1, 1943

> From: Major Donald E. Mathes, Headquarters 14th Battalion
> Armored Force Replacement Training Center
> Fort Knox, Kentucky
>
> I had the pleasure of seeing Hugh DeAutremont during
> November 1942 for the first time since 1923, and I was hap-
> py to find him in good spirits, his morale not broken, and
> anxious to repay his debt to society.
>
> I would be pleased to have him in my Battalion and I
> have no doubt that he can again be as good a soldier as
> formerly was and prove to be a fine man. He was a good
> boy in our home town and I know he can fight.
>
> He deeply regrets his one mistake and will gladly give
> his life if necessary to serve his country.
>
> Again, I wish to state I would be glad to have him sent to
> my Battalion and I will personally be responsible for his
> actions.
>
> If the Government needs character witnesses, I feel sure
> any of his former teachers or class mates in high school will
> back him to the limit.
>
> I have always felt as though I would like to see Hugh
> since he got into that trouble and now after seeing him and
> talking to him, I am more than ever sold on him and I feel
> that he is ready to be given a chance to prove to the world
> that he still has got what it takes.

Psychiatric report on Hugh:

> Report to the Parole Board on Hugh DeAutremont, prisoner
> # 9902
> From John W. Evans, M.D., 919 Taylor Street Bldg.,
> Portland, Oregon . . . . . September 8, 1947

When I was associated with the Parole Board as psychiatric
consultant in 1940, I examined an inmate at the Oregon State
Penitentiary, one, Hugh DeAutremont. His examination was in
part a routine matter for many life-termers who were brought up
before the board at that time. The up-shot of the psychiatric examination at that time was the fact that we were dealing with a
long-term prisoner who had remained relatively intact from the
standpoint of personal function and it was my feeling and the feeling of some others that the man himself was ready for return to
society.

The possibility of his release was considered only to be quickly
rejected, not because of the man's status but because of

1. Release would mean his serving time in Federal Penitentiary.
2. Release might mean indictment for a second count in
   Josephine (author's note; should be Jackson County) County.
3. Railroads would bring pressure to bear.

4. Popular opinion would be against the release of the notorious criminal.
5. The Board was new and had not gained the confidence of the community.
6. The governor was in first term and probably would not care to be involved in such an issue.

Since returning from the service, I have visited Mr. DeAutremont on one occasion and he appears to be relatively intact; however, I do not know about this for sure. At any rate, I felt morally bound as an individual to do a little foot work on this case because I feel it spotlights the theme that when a prisoner can be considered to be rehabilitated and safe for society he should be released regardless of prejudices, etc. In other words, I am not particularly interested in the personality involved here but am definitely interested in advertising the above sociologic precept.

In the last week a number of things have been done and I wish to report them to you:

1. Mrs. John Catlin visited the head of the S. P. railroad in San Francisco who informed her that the railroads would certainly not stand in the way of action in this case. He did add that there was a man in Portland who had been with the railroads in the 20's who still felt rather strongly about the matter but that anything this man would say would be unofficial.
2. Mr. Twining, Assistant U. S. Attorney, was contacted and stated that Federal Indictment probably would not be pressed if the Federal people were satisfied with the release situation after they had reviewed it. He stated that it is the custom of the Federal Government to drop such old indictments if the State has declared a man in good condition.
3. Contacted Catholic chaplain at the prison who feels that release is indicated.
4. Contacted Mr. Humphrey, Assistant Editor of the Journal, who feels that his paper would use news of release in a constructive, sociologic manner and would not use it for its notoriety value.
5. Mr. Parrish of the Oregonian felt that his editorial policy would be formed if and when something happened. He would not commit himself, but one felt that he would be favorably inclined to use such a case in a constructive social way rather than to play on the prejudices of the people.
6. I was unable to contact the District Attorney at Grants Pass (author's note: should be Medford) to discuss with him the attitude of his county. Obviously this should be done but I fear that I shall not be able to do it.

I talked with Mr. Mason who suggested that I put this data in your hands for what it is worth.

Many pleas were made on behalf of the prisoners:

Letter to the Parole Board on Hugh DeAutremont, prisoner #9902, dated November 16, 1948

From: Mrs. Edward C. Kelly
       906 West Fourth Street
       Medford, Oregon

This is to respectfully ask your consideration of a parole for

Hugh D'Autremont, who has now served twenty-one years of a life sentence in the state penitentiary, for his part in the Siskiyou tunnel murder of 1923. It is my understanding that under a recently enacted law, it is possible, upon good behavior, to be eligible for a parole after eight years of such a sentence has been served.

The Oregon constitution specifically provides that the object of imprisonment shall be reformation not punishment. The devotion of enlightened boards of parole and probation to rehabilitation and reformation, plus the plain mandate of the Oregon constitution, which they are sworn to uphold, seems to call for careful consideration of this particular case. Otherwise, after 21 years of imprisonment, what incentive is there left, if a man, who has worked as zealously as Hugh D'Autremont, to prove himself, couldn't be given consideration for parole?

It is my information, that during the more than two decades he has served, there has never been any inmate with a higher record for behavior and performance. As editor of the prison publication, Shadows, and more recently, in complete charge of the institution's printing, he has proved himself capable of taking responsibility, guiding and directing others, and turning his talents to worthwhile account. In a recent interview with him he expressed particular pride and gratification that he and his staff had handled the printing for so many charitable and philanthropic drives such as the Tubercular Seal Sales, children's homes and schools, etc. This indicates, I feel, a right attitude toward community responsibility.

As a newspaper reporter I covered the D'Autremont trial in 1927, have made my home in the community ever since, and am perhaps as well acquainted as anyone, not only with the complete background acd circumstances, but with all the personalities involved in the case. While the D'Autremont case, because of its wide publicity, stands out in the public mind, still this, in itself should not be a factor in withholding just recognition for such a long period of exceptionally good behavior. Also, in the background of the crime itself, were circumstances, I feel, should be taken into consideration by the parole board in reviewing the case of Hugh D'Autremont.

The De'Autremont boys (there were five of them altogether) were the victims of a broken home, the father, after much restless moving around the country, having left the mother to battle it out alone in the God-forsaken desert town of Lakewood, New Mexico. There she did her best to make a home and eke out a living for her five, by running a little general merchandise store.

Dissatisfied, the two oldest boys, the twins, Ray and Roy, finally followed their father up north into Oregon, seeking work. They found the father had remarrried and had inherited a ready-made family of small children to support, so there was no home for them. This, coupled with their inability to find work over a considerable period of time, embittered Ray particularly, and he became obsessed with some erratic, socialistic thinking. He was extremely persuasive and gradually talked his brother Roy into the notion that the world owed them a living, even if they had to violate some laws to get it.

It was at this time that the two of them came back and got Hugh, then just 18 and out of high school, and took him north with them to "look for work". From then on, he was definitely under the influence and domination of his two older brothers (four years his senior) until after that nightmare of a crime had been committed.

The subject's extreme youth at the time, coupled with his record of fine behavior on all other occasions isolated from this one incident, certainly indicates that he is inherently a good and sound individual. Even following the crime, he served two years in the United States Army in the Phillipines making a good record and receiving a promotion.

Because of his long period of punishment, his excellent institutional record, the concrete proof of his reformation and right attitude, and because he is equipped by training and intelligence to take his place in society, I ask your board to give this prisoner your just consideration for parole.

Report to the Parole Board on Hugh DeAutremont, prisoner #9902, from Robert A. Coen, M.D. . . . . .April 26, 1949

Briefly this prisoner's psychiatric status at the present time remains without significant change since 1940. He is now 45 and in good physical health. He considers himself a little moody but no significant swings in mood. He feels that he makes a very good adjustment with people, that he forms and maintains close personal attachments. At the same time, he feels some restraint and is never enthusiastic nor given to back-slapping tactics. He feels that other people in turn treat him well, probably much better than he deserves.

At times he is a little on edge, and for this reason prefers in general to keep busy. However, he points out that the tasks he accomplishes must be tasks that he likes, for he rebels against doing distasteful procedures. He read much until recent years, at which time he began developing eye problems.

He sees his one brother, Roy, frequently, feels the same attachment for him. His brother, Ray, Hugh states, has developed mental difficulties (author's note: The Doctor has the twins reversed here as it was Roy who had developed mental difficulties, but this is something which many people and articles did, which occasionally added difficulty to research) and remains interested, however, in seeing if there isn't some sort of medical aid that could be given to Ray.

He holds to precisely the same story described to Dr. Evans. One cannot doubt the veracity of this story. Although the crime was notorious, bloody, and in many of its aspects, outstandingly horrible, nevertheless, from the standpoint of this prisoner Hugh, the intense bond existing between the brothers is a definite contributing factor. It is strange that loyalty could lead to the commission of such an act.

When the family moved from Colorado to New Mexico, they were looked on as foreigners, and the children all treated as though they were strange individuals. The brothers were drawn together, therefore, not only by the ambitions of the mother, but by some of the common difficult elements in the environment.

The financial standing of the family was so consistently poor, particularly after left stranded by the father and emphasized by the illness of a younger brother who had tuberculosis of the hip, that there remained a consistent necessity for more funds.

Hugh had worked his way through school, had stayed out two years to work on different occasions, had become rather discouraged, but finally managed to complete his education. Ray, working in Oregon and apparently of somewhat different personality make-up from the others, first conceived the idea of crime, not specifically, but generally for financial return. He persisted, persuaded Roy, and the two of them eventually persuaded Hugh.

It is important to note that this was entirely against the principles of Hugh, that he was forced to weigh loyalty to his brothers against the commission of a criminal act. He reached the point that he felt hopeless, blue, and had a sense of impending catastrophe. He was less able to offer arguments, and gradually his resistance melted before what proved the stronger factor in his motivations.

This man is highly intelligent, definitely sincere, slightly tense, an introvert, reserved, well integrated, and remorseful of an act committed. He feels actually that he began to serve time from the moment Ray first suggested the idea to him, for he felt penitence and an insult to all his ideals from that time on.

He is slightly tense, presents a mild tremor of the facial muscles. There are no abnormal mental trends. His basic personality falls within normal limits. From a psychiatric standpoint, it is considered that this man presents a reasonably good parole risk for the following reasons:

1. There is no evidence of psychopathic make-up or unpatterned behavior.
2. Conscience has existed and restrained activity well except in the presence of personal factors brought to bear with an extremely high degree of family relationship pressure.
3. Prison adjustment has been excellent.
4. This man has been consistently penitent and remains so.
5. There is, therefore, evidence medically that this man's personality make-up is such that there would be no danger of antisocial activity in the future.

It should be emphasized that the examiner is not trying to offer any excuse for the crime committed. It is easy to misinterpret the above statements. The only point of value is that there are restraining influences in this man which assure one he is not a danger to society.

The fact cannot be overlooked, of course, that if this man were released, he would no doubt be tried again and possibly sentenced to death or at least returned to prison for life again. There is, therefore, no recommendation made.

Many people were interested in Hugh having the opportunity for parole:

Letter to the Parole Board on behalf of
Hugh DeAutremont . . . . dated May 7, 1949

From: Rev. Robert S. Neugebauer
Visitation Church
Route 2, Box 110
Forest Grove, Oregon

On behalf of Mr. Hugh D'Autremont of the Oregon State Penitentary I wish to send this note of recommendation. I understand he will soon face the Parole Board to have his case and long record of good conducts reviewed, for the purpose of determining a possible parole.

I first met Mr. Hugh D'Autremont some fourteen years ago, when I assumed the post as the Catholic Chaplain of the Oregon State Penitentiary. I served in that capacity for two and one half years. During that time and since I have had many contacts with Mr. D'Autremont and have become very well acquainted with him. I always found him very steady, dependable, courteous and honest. I am firmly convinced too that he has long since realized the heinousness of his crimes, and within himself has truly repented. Now, he wants to show the world he has repented, by living a useful, honest, honorable life therein. Whether or not he has paid his debt to Society by his confinement in the Penitentiary these many years, and whether or not he would be accepted in Society, of course, are questions for which you no doubt have better answers than I. My personal opinion, however, is that he has, and I think would become a useful citizen in any Community.

He also knows he will have to readjust himself if he gets his parole; that he will encounter many humiliations, accusations and the guffaw of mean people, as well as being the object of suspicion, until he proves himself, and in my opinion, I believe he will be able to cope with all these things very nobly.

Will you therefore give him your honest consideration at least for his many years of good behavior, in spite of the crimes that caused him confinement behind the walls of the Penitentiary.

Index